CURSE
REVERSED

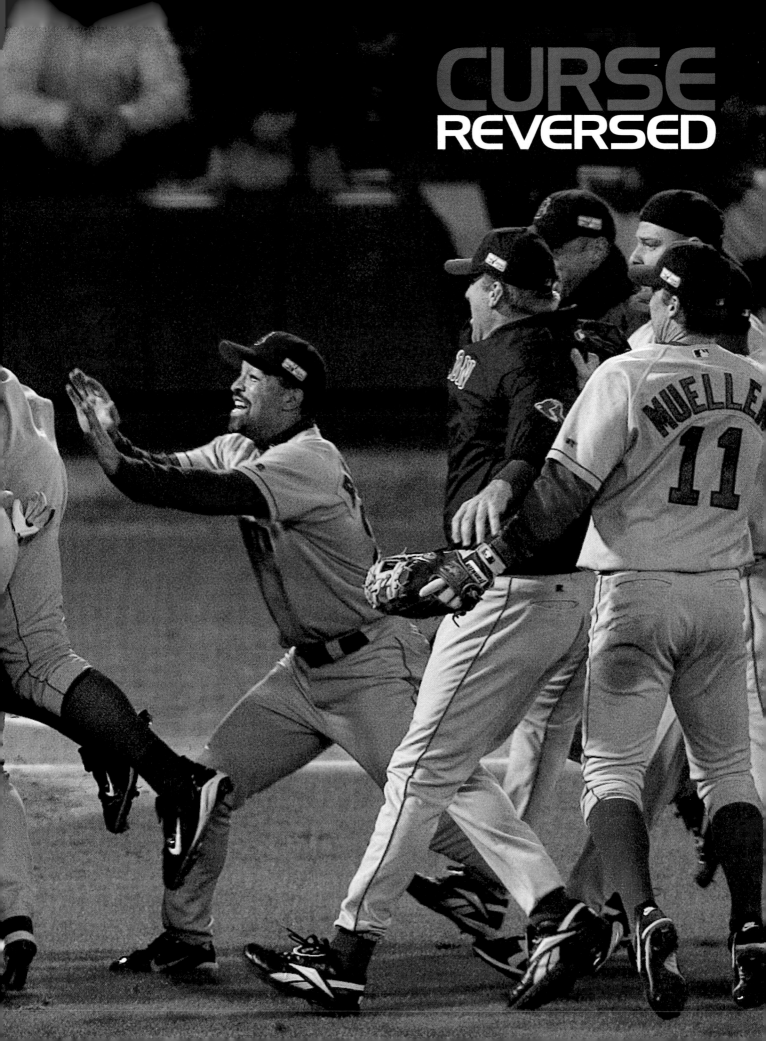

CURSE
REVERSED

Designed by Bob Parajon ◆ **Edited by Ron Smith** ◆ **Written by Stan McNeal, Kyle Veltrop**

Contributing writers: Chris Bahr, Mike Kilduff, Ron Smith, Dale Bye.

Photo editors: Michael McNamara, Paul Nisely.

Copy editors: John Rawlings, Dave Sloan, Joe Hoppel, Corrie Anderson, Jim Gilstrap, Matt Crossman, Kyle Veltrop.

Cover design: Chad Painter, Bill Wilson.

Page design: Bob Parajon, Michael Behrens, Angie Pillman.

Prepress specialists: Steve Romer, Pamela Speh, Russ Carr, Vern Kasal.

PHOTO CREDITS

T = Top, B = Bottom, R = Right, L = Left, M = Middle

Sporting News Archives: 8, 9, 10, 11, 20

AP/Wide World Photos: Front cover, back cover, 6, 7(5), 14, 15, 22T, 23T, 23B, 24L, 25, 26, 27, 28T, 28B, 29T, 29BL, 29BR, 30T, 30B, 31B, 31T, 32, 33, 34T, 34B, 35T, 35M, 35R, 37(5), 38, 39, 40, 41(5), 42 (2), 43(4), 44, 45, 46, 47(2), 48(2), 49(3), 54(3), 56, 57, 58(2), 59(3), 60, 61, 62(2), 63(6), 68T, 72TL, 72TR, 73BL, 73BM, 73BR, 74R, 78TL, 81BL, 81BR, 82, 83, 84BL, 85(2), 86BL, 87B, 92ML, 95, 97MR, 98(3), 99MR, 116, 117, 118T, 119 120BL, 121B, 131BR, 144

Robert Seale/TSN: 108, 109, 110(3), 111(4), 112TL, 112TR, 113L, 114TL, 114M, 115TR, 120BR, 121TL, 123BL, 123BR, 124, 125, 126BL, 130TL, 130BR, 135, 136TR, 136BR, 138(3), 139TL, 139TR,

Albert Dickson/TSN: 16, 17, 18, 19, 126BR, 129(3), 131TR, 131BL, 134BL, 136BL,

Jay Drowns/TSN: 5, 76, 77, 78BL, 79(6), 80(3), 81TL, 81TR, 82T, 84T, 84BR, 86TL, 86TR, 86BR, 87TL, 87TR, 88, 89, 90(2), 91(4), 92(6), 93(3), 94, 112B, 114BL, 114-115, 115BR, 118B, 120T, 121TR, 122, 123T, 123TR

Michael McNamara/TSN: 2-3, 126TL, 127TR, 128(2), 130BL, 130TM, 131ML, 132, 133, 134TL, 137, 139B,

John Cordes for TSN: 52, 53, 55(4),

John Dunn for TSN: 64, 65, 66, 67(5), 68L, 68R, 69(5), 70(2), 71, 72M, 72B, 74L, 75(3), 96(3), 97TL, 97(3), 99(7), 100, 101, 102(3), 103(4) 104(4), 105(4), 113R

Al Bello/Getty Images: 21, 22B

Ezra Shaw/Getty Images: 12R, 13ML, 24T, 24B, 36

ISBN: 0-89204-780-1   10 9 8 7 6 5 4 3 2 1

CONTENTS

INTRODUCTION

First, let's get one thing clear: No one, not even the staunchest Red Sox fan, talked about the Curse of the Bambino during the Roaring Twenties or during the Depression or while World War II was raging. It also didn't come up in 1946 when the St. Louis Cardinals snatched Game 7 of the 1946 World Series on Country Slaughter's Mad Dash around the bases while Johnny Pesky held the ball.

There still was no mention of any Curse when the Red Sox fell again to the Cardinals in a World Series, this time in 1967. In fact, that season was known in Boston as The Impossible Dream.

But after the Red Sox lost the 1975 World Series, despite Carlton Fisk positively willing that home run fair, and the galling loss to the New York Mets in the 1986 World Series—that's where Bill Buckner comes in—this Curse thing had taken root deep in New England lore.

Every kid in New England—and every Sox fan from Boston to Bangor to Belfast to Baghdad—knows the story …

How the Red Sox, with Babe Ruth and Harry Hooper and Carl Mays, won the 1918 World Series. How owner Harry Frazee needed money to finance "No, No Nanette," a Broadway musical. How Frazee sold Ruth's contract to the New York Yankees for $125,000. How the Yankees went on to become the most dominant franchise of the 20th century and how the Red Sox never again won a World Series.

So there you have it. The "No, No Nanette" part has been pretty much discredited, but the rest of it is fact. Especially this part: From 1919 through 2003, the Red Sox, winners of five of the first 15 World Series, captured not a single Series championship. Sometimes the Red Sox were plain lousy; sometimes the pitching was good and the Red Sox couldn't score; more often, the team had the thumpers but the pitching stunk, and always there were the damn Yankees (even the Pilgrims would have called them that) getting in the way. There was Bucky #*&@ing Dent and Aaron #*&@ing Boone and any number of other pinstriped hobgoblins gnawing at the New England psyche.

And that's how things stood on Sunday morning, October 17, Year of the Curse 86. The Yankees had just beaten the Red Sox, 19-8, taking a 3-0 lead in the American League Championship Series. No baseball team had ever come back and won a seven-game postseason series after losing the first three, so that was that, and the Curse was the Curse for another year.

Except the Red Sox won that night (and into the next morning) in 12 innings.

And they won the next game, which lasted 14 innings. And the next game. And another—four straight over the Yankees.

A miracle? No less than that, certainly.

An Impossible Dream? Those fans back in '67 had no idea.

The Cardinals came to Boston for the World Series, and the Red Sox won the first game—despite committing four errors.

And they won the second—despite committing four errors.

Cursed? Not this self-proclaimed Band of Idiots.

In St. Louis, the Red Sox finished the sweep. No more errors. No more dramatics. Sox fans—although they never really quite believed it—never had a single occasion to even hold their breath.

Believe it!

The Curse? Swept away.

The Yankees? Kicked to the side.

It was a memorable climax to a memorable Red Sox season—one that brought tears to grandfathers and fathers and sons alike.

This time, those were tears of joy.

RED SOX *Champions*

1903 Burying two years of hostility between the established National League and fledgling American League, Pittsburgh owner Barney Dreyfuss and Boston's Henry Killilea agreed late in the 1903 season to stage a best-of-nine postseason playoff series for the "world championship" of baseball. The Red Sox needed only eight of those games to upset the Pirates in the first modern World Series and give the A.L. a much-needed dose of credibility.

The Red Sox delivered a lethal 1-2 punch in the form of pitchers Cy Young and Bill Dinneen, who pitched 69 of 71 innings and posted all five of their wins after the Red Sox lost a 7-3 Series opener to Pittsburgh workhorse Deacon Phillippe. Dinneen recorded three wins, including a 3-0 Game 8 clincher in which second baseman Hobe Ferris drove in all of Boston's runs.

Young won twice and recorded a 1.59 ERA while Phillippe, a three-game winner for Pittsburgh, worked an amazing 44 innings in five games. The Pirates won three of the first four games before Boston reeled off four straight wins to close them out.

Jimmy Collins' Boston team (below), led by pitching great Denton 'Cy' Young, claimed an eight-game victory over N.L.-champion Pittsburgh in the first modern World Series in 1903. By 1912, the World Series had become an annual affair that drew many fans to a large New York message board (left) to receive game information of their Giants' fall classic battle against the Red Sox. Boston won its second championship that year.

Tris Speaker (left) helped the Red Sox bring a World Series winner to new Fenway Park (right) in 1912. Duffy Lewis (below) was a .444 hitter in Boston's 1915 Series win over the Phillies.

1912 The Red Sox (105 wins) and Giants (103) cruised to pennants, setting up a classic World Series that was not decided until the 10th inning of the Game 8 finale. Boston won when Tris Speaker's single and Larry Gardner's sacrifice fly produced two runs after the Giants had scored in the top of the inning on Fred Merkle's single.

The Red Sox's Series-ending rally was aided by two Giants' misplays. The first batter in the 10th, Clyde Engle, reached second base when center fielder Fred Snodgrass inexplicably dropped his routine fly ball. Engle scored the tying run when Speaker, given new life when his foul pop fell untouched between first baseman Merkle and catcher Chief Meyers, delivered his single off hard-luck loser Christy Mathewson and set up Gardner's winning fly ball.

Smokey Joe Wood, who posted 34 regular-season victories, pitched the last three innings of the finale to earn his third win in a Series that included a 6-6 tie.

1915 A Red Sox team that won 101 games, only one more than Detroit in the American League, needed five World Series games to dispose of the Phillies, a team that had won 11 fewer regular-season games while

The 1915 pitching staff of (left to right) Rube Foster, Carl Mays, Ernie Shore, Babe Ruth and Dutch Leonard led the Sox to a championship. It wasn't until 1918 that Ruth saw more extended postseason action as a hitter.

cruising to a National League pennant.

Grover Cleveland Alexander pitched the Phillies to a 3-1 victory over the Red Sox in the Series opener at tiny Baker Bowl, but the Red Sox reeled off four straight wins behind the pitching of Eddie Shore, Rube Foster and Dutch Leonard and the blazing bat of left fielder Duffy Lewis, who compiled a .444 average and homered in Boston's 5-4 Game 5 clincher. All of the Red Sox's "home games" were played at new Braves Field instead of Fenway Park because of its superior seating capacity.

Young lefthander Babe Ruth, an 18-game regular-season winner, made only one appearance in his first World Series—as a pinch hitter in the ninth inning of Game 1. Ruth grounded out against Alexander.

1916 Bill Carrigan's Red Sox became the third team to repeat as World Series champion and the first to win four fall classics as they dispatched the Brooklyn Dodgers in five games. The key victory came in Game 2 when Babe Ruth, a 23-game regular-season winner with an American League-leading 1.75 ERA, outdueled Sherry Smith, 2-1, in a 14-inning thriller.

Boston, which had won the opener behind Eddie Shore, wouldn't need Ruth again. The Red Sox lost, 4-3, in Game 3, but bounced back for a 6-2 win behind Dutch Leonard and a 4-1 clinching victory behind Shore, who allowed only three hits. Third baseman Larry Gardner supplied plenty of muscle with two home runs and six RBIs for the winning Sox.

Ruth batted five times in his Game 2 marathon effort, but failed to collect his first World Series hit. He did drive in his first run with a groundout.

1918 With Babe Ruth seeing his first extended action as a combination outfielder-pitcher, the Red Sox outdueled Cleveland in a World War I-shortened regular season and the Chicago Cubs in a six-game World Series. Ruth, who had tied for the A.L. home run lead with 11, did more damage with his arm in the fall classic, posting two victories and a 1.06 ERA over 17 innings.

Ruth was at his best in Game 1 when he outdueled Chicago's Hippo Vaughn in a 1-0 thriller. But he wasn't bad in Game 4, either, working eight innings and posting a 3-2 win that gave the Red Sox a three-games-to-one advantage and collecting his first Series hit, a triple.

Carl Mays took care of the Game 6 clincher, pitching the Red Sox to a 2-1 win and lifting their record to 5-0 in World Series play. The Series, in which neither team scored more than three runs in any game, was played from September 5-11 because of war-time restrictions.

Dutch Leonard, an 18-game winner during the regular season, gave the Red Sox a three-games-to-one advantage in the 1916 World Series when he posted a 6-2 win over the Brooklyn Dodgers.

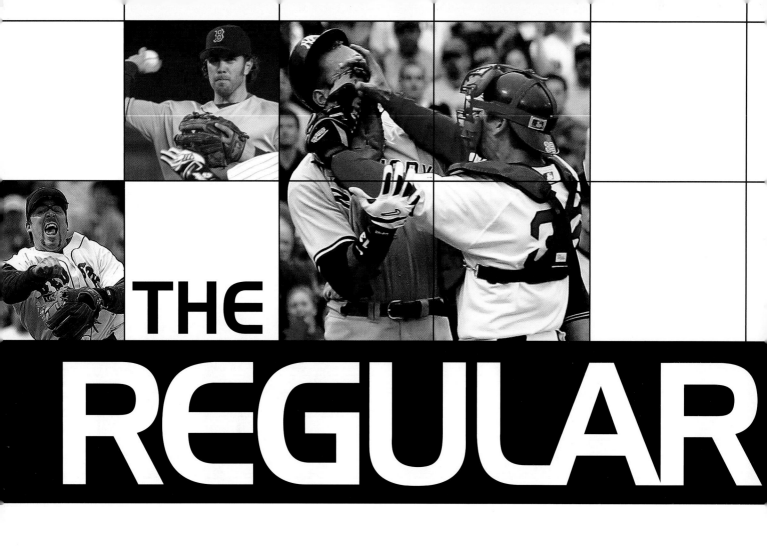

THE REGULAR

Eyeball to eyeball.

From the beginning of the 2004 season—wait a minute, from the moment Aaron Boone's home run left Yankee Stadium to end the 2003 season for the Red Sox—one thing was clear: The 2004 American League pennant—and probably the World Series champion—was going to be decided inside baseball's best and fiercest rivalry.

Which team would be better, the Yankees or the Red Sox?

Eyeball to eyeball.

The duel began in the offseason, and every move was made with one thing in mind. The six regular-season series with the Yankees were only a prelude—an intense prelude, of course, but still a prelude—to what every Red Sox fan knew was coming in October: a seven-game series against the Yankees to determine the American League champion.

Eyeball to eyeball.

The first round began April 16 at Fenway Park …

SEASON

Sox do Monster mash as the rivalry resumes

Alex Rodriguez got a taste of baseball's best rivalry only hours before he stepped into Fenway Park for the first time as a member of the Yankees. He was lunching at a downtown restaurant when a local strolled by, recognized the Yankees' new third baseman and promptly gave him a middle-finger salute.

Welcome to Boston, A-Rod.

The Sox had come close to trading for Rodriguez in the offseason but couldn't close the deal. Soon after, George Steinbrenner swooped in and added the game's most celebrated player to a lineup already considered among the best in the game. The A-Rod acquisition completed an offseason game of "OK, top this" by the two clubs.

Since the Yankees had devastated Red Sox Nation with a seven-game A.L. Championship Series triumph the previous October, the clubs had continued their competition in the hot-stove league. The Yankees signed Gary Sheffield, traded for starters Kevin Brown and Javier Vazquez and added reliever Tom Gordon.

The Sox came up short in the A-Rod sweepstakes, but still improved themselves significantly. They traded for righthander Curt Schilling, who had shut down the Yankees three times for the Arizona Diamondbacks in the 2001 World Series, and, just as important, signed closer Keith Foulke a year after their failed experience with a closer-by-committee approach.

Anticipation for the first 2004 series between the clubs was even greater than usual, a strong statement considering it always has been one of the most intense matchups in sports. The first spring training game matching the teams attracted so many

Curt Schilling, making his first visit to Boston since signing with the Red Sox, stands in front of his new locker at Fenway Park. Derek Jeter (above right) helps Alex Rodriguez try on his new pinstripes as manager Joe Torre looks on during a February news conference at Yankee Stadium.

October 29, 2003: The Red Sox put Ramirez on irrevocable waivers, but he goes unclaimed.

November 28, 2003: Schilling and the Red Sox reach a deal in principle that will send him from Arizona to Boston.

December 4, 2003: Francona is hired as manager, replacing Grady Little.

2004 Final Records
Yankees, 101-61; Red Sox, 98-64 (Red Sox won series, 11-8)

fans to the Sox's Florida home in Fort Myers that tickets reportedly were scalped for several times their face value. And Fox Sports bought into the hype by making the Friday night series opener its first prime-time regular-season baseball telecast since 1998, when Mark McGwire hit his record 62nd home run. Even though both teams started their seasons sluggishly, the 5-4 Yankees still came to town in first place, one-half game ahead of the Red Sox.

When the four-game set ended with the annual Patriot's Day matinee, the Sox had jumped ahead of them. Playing in front of sellout crowds, as they would every home game all season, the Red Sox won three of the four games behind a pitching staff that limited the Yankees to eight runs. Schilling earned a win in his first Fenway start and Foulke was on the mound for the last out of all three victories.

Offensively, the Red Sox's bashers took turns providing heroics. Third baseman Bill Mueller, the reigning A.L. batting champ, had at least one hit in every game and finished 8-for-15. He was 3-for-3 with a homer in support of Tim Wakefield in the Friday night opener, a game in which Manny Ramirez also homered as the Red Sox jumped out quickly to a 4-0 first-inning lead. Ramirez hit his 350th career homer the next day in support of Schilling, who allowed one run in 6⅓ innings before giving way to the bullpen. Designated hitter David Ortiz's two run-scoring singles helped the Red Sox overcome a 4-1 deficit in a 5-4 fourth-game win.

The Yankees' only victory came against sinkerballer Derek Lowe, who was pounded for seven runs in 2⅔ innings of the third game. The middle of the order did most of the damage in a six-run third when Sheffield, Hideki Matsui, Jorge Posada and Bernie Williams all had RBI hits. Righthander Jose Contreras started but lasted only

Tim Wakefield (above) allowed just four hits in seven innings of Game 1—his first game against the Yankees since giving up Aaron Boone's game-winning homer in the 2003 ALCS. Manny Ramirez is congratulated by Kevin Millar after homering.

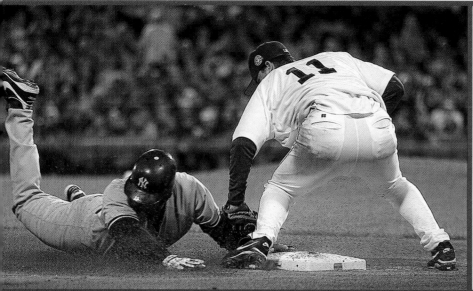

It was a tough first series for Alex Rodriguez, who was thrown out trying to steal in Game 1 (left) and did not get a hit until the ninth inning of the series finale—much to the delight of the Fenway faithful. Boston's Bill Mueller was hot, going 8-for-15 with a Game 1 homer (below left), and Keith Foulke (getting a handshake from catcher Doug Mirabelli) was on the mound for the last out of all three Red Sox wins.

December 13, 2003: Foulke signs with Boston, ending the "bullpen by committee" debacle of 2003.

December 16, 2003: The Red Sox acquire Bellhorn from the Rockies.

December 23, 2003: The deal for A-Rod officially dies.

2⅓ innings. Relievers Paul Quantrill, Gabe White, Gordon and Mariano Rivera shut out the Sox over the final 6⅔ innings of a 7-3 victory.

Wakefield, the knuckleballer who served up Aaron Boone's pennant-winning home run in the 2003 ALCS, limited the Yankees to two runs in seven innings of the opener. A favorite of Red Sox fans, Wakefield was treated to a standing ovation when he left the game—a show of support for the previous fall as much as appreciation of his winning performance.

"They really have opened their arms and embraced me like their second son," Wakefield said. "I take a lot of pride in saying I'm a Red Sox player."

While Schilling and Foulke enjoyed their first experience as part of the Sox-Yankees rivalry, Yankees newcomers did not fare so well. Sheffield went 3-for-15 in the four games and Brown left his fourth-game start with a 4-3 lead, only to watch the bullpen fail to hold it.

No one, however, struggled more than A-Rod, who went hitless until there were two out in the ninth inning of the final game. His average when he left town: .160. After each game, more than a dozen reporters packed around his locker seeking explanations. After each game, A-Rod patiently answered questions. He felt good. He was so close to breaking out. It felt good to slam his helmet down after making yet another out.

"He's human," Yankees manager Joe Torre said. "He's going through a tough time now, playing for a tough ball club in a city that doesn't ease up on the tension.

"I think there's still an adjustment period he's going through. It sort of piles on more responsibility, which obviously doesn't make it easy. But there's nothing we can do for him. He's going to have to work his way through it."

There was a long season ahead to do just that.

Schilling shined in his first start against his new rival. The big righthander pitched into the seventh inning, striking out eight and allowing only one run. Ramirez pounded a homer—the 350th of his career—in Game 2.

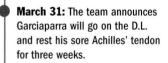

March 31: The team announces Garciaparra will go on the D.L. and rest his sore Achilles' tendon for three weeks.

April 1: Reports surface that Martinez has ended negotiations to extend his Red Sox contract.

April 4: Martinez loses the season opener to the Orioles, creating panic in Beantown.

Although the Yankees scored early and often on Derek Lowe (above) in Game 3, the Sox were able to win three of four games at Fenway Park, thanks to the gritty play of such players as (clockwise from left) Johnny Damon, Bill Mueller and Pokey Reese.

Red Sox sweep aside struggling Yankees

The game opened with typical Red Sox-Yankees venom. The Yankee Stadium crowd of 55,001 began an obscene anti-Boston chant with the first pitch and every Pedro Martinez move, every Manny Ramirez swing was greeted with a torrent of boos and other invectives. But several hours later, jeering chants of "Let's Go Red Sox" knifed through the Stadium and postgame talk centered on a stunning Red Sox sweep and the boos that were directed at New York icon Derek Jeter and other flailing Yankee stars.

"We would have booed ourselves tonight," said Jeter, who had gone 0-for-13 and struck out six times in the three-game series while running his hitless streak to a career-long 25 at-bats. "It's hard to imagine being worse than we were. Put me on the front of that list."

But not alone. Check these early season averages: Bernie Williams .167, Jason Giambi .204, Ruben Sierra .194, Enrique Wilson .167 and Alex Rodriguez .257, an average that was actually on the rise after the dreadful series that had ended four days earlier at Fenway Park.

The Yankees' misfortune mirrored the Red Sox's early success. With Martinez's 2-0 win in the Sunday series finale, the Red Sox completed their first sweep of the Yankees since 1999 and improved their record against them to 6-1. They left New York with a 4½-game lead in the A.L. East Division and the Yankees three games under .500 for the first time since April 1997.

"It's great—as many wins off them as we can get," Red Sox center fielder Johnny Damon said after an 11-2 series-opening blowout. "We know they are going to be there at the end, so we're going to enjoy this while we can. Hopefully, they don't hit for a while longer, and we can get out of town before they do."

The series started with Derek Lowe in top form and the Red Sox scoring

Alex Rodriguez (left) and Derek Jeter try to help Jose Contreras (holding hat) figure out what went wrong against the Red Sox, who rocked him for five runs and two home runs—including one by Mark Bellhorn—in an 11-2 series-opening Boston victory.

April 21: A sign of things to come: Mirabelli homers twice and drives in three runs in a win over the Blue Jays.

April 28: In a 6-0 win over Tampa Bay, Schilling takes a line drive off his right foot, the beginning, perhaps, of his later ankle problems.

April 29: Boston is 15-6 with a three-game lead over the Orioles and a 4½-game lead over the Yankees.

early and often. They hit four home runs—Bill Mueller, Ramirez, Kevin Millar and Mark Bellhorn—and piled up 12 hits off four pitchers whose names would not be called in October—starter Jose Contreras, Donovan Osborne, Scott Proctor and Alex Graman.

Lowe, who had been pounded by the Yankees in the first series at Boston, gave up just two earned runs in six innings and left with a 10-2 lead. His trademark sinker was sharp as the Yankees made only three outs on balls hit in the air. The eighth, ninth and leadoff hitters in the Red Sox lineup—Bellhorn, Pokey Reese and Damon—combined for seven hits, six runs and five RBIs. But Mueller's three-run homer broke the game open in the fourth.

On Saturday, Rodriguez enjoyed his first big game in front of his new home crowd—he slugged a home run and scored both runs—but the Red Sox still won, 3-2, in 12 innings. Four Sox relievers—Scott Williamson, Alan Embree, Keith Foulke and Mike Timlin—ran the bullpen's scoreless streak to 22⅔ innings by shutting out the Yankees from the seventh inning on. A bright spot for the Yankees was the continued strong early season performance of Kevin Brown, who held the Sox to two runs in seven innings and dropped his ERA to 2.12.

The winning run scored when Bellhorn drove in Ramirez with a sacrifice fly, the Sox's third of the game. Martinez was in control on Sunday, when he blanked the Yankees on four hits over seven innings. Martinez's shutout was secured by Williamson with a perfect eighth and ninth. Martinez was brilliant, mixing a wicked curve and changeup with his fastball. Of his seven strikeouts, five were on called third strikes. His signature moment came in the fifth inning when he escaped a second-and-third, one-out jam by getting Wilson on a popup and striking out Jeter looking.

Mark Bellhorn, known primarily as a hard-hitting second baseman, participated in three double plays in the first two games of the series against the Yankees.

Bill Mueller, the A.L.'s 2003 batting champ, connects with a pitch from Donovan Osborne for a first-game, fourth-inning, three-run homer.

The Red Sox were out of reach for Derek Jeter and the Yanks through a difficult weekend. The 11-2 first-game victory provided sweet revenge for Derek Lowe.

May 8: Reese, acquired in the offseason for his defense, homers twice in a 9-1 win over K.C.

May 10: Arroyo replaces Kim as the fifth starter. Kim is sent to Class AAA Pawtucket.

"(The mood of the team) is not too good," Yankees manager Joe Torre said after watching his team fall to 8-11. "But I'd be worried about them if they were in there having a good time."

Across the way, the mood was decidedly better—but short of ecstatic. "We're happy," Damon said, "but I wish we could go back to that (2003 ALCS) Game 7 and make these games count instead. Like they always say in Boston, this is our year. We've shown it so far. This does a lot for our confidence."

Bronson Arroyo (top right) allowed only one hit through six innings of the second game, setting the stage for Manny Ramirez (right) to double and score the winning run on a 12th-inning sacrifice fly. Shortstop Pokey Reese contributed defensively by participating in two double plays.

May 15: Youkilis homers in his first game with the Red Sox.

May 20: Ortiz agrees to a two-year contract extension.

May 20: Damon shaves his now-infamous beard for charity. He immediately grows it back, to the delight of "Damon's Disciples."

Pedro Martinez had reason to smile in his first trip back to Yankee Stadium since the fateful Game 7 of the 2003 ALCS. He pitched seven shutout innings and the Red Sox completed their sweep with a 2-0 victory.

25

Yankees turn tables with sweeping flair

Anyone who booed Derek Jeter in April would not admit it in July. No way. Especially if they saw the catch he made against the Red Sox on the night of July 1.

The Yankees captain has built his career around big plays, but longtime observers said this one is surpassed only by the flip play he made in the 2001 A.L. Division Series against the Athletics. Jeter's catch showed off his many qualities: speed, athletic ability and, most of all, heart. With two out and the score tied in the 12th inning of a game Red Sox center fielder Johnny Damon called an "instant classic," the Red Sox had runners on second and third when Trot Nixon hit a short pop to left field.

Left fielder Ruben Sierra was not going to get it. Neither was third baseman Alex Rodriguez. But Jeter would not be denied. Running full speed toward the seats beyond third base, he made the catch and, unable to stop or even slow down, launched himself head-first over a short wall and into the stands. He was parallel to the ground as his face and right shoulder crunched into the seats. He got up slowly, his face bloodied and the ball in his glove. As he made his way to the Yankees dugout, assisted by a trainer, he flipped the ball to a kid near the third base dugout. Anyone who saw the catch will not forget it.

Alex Rodriguez called it the greatest he had ever witnessed. "He went in so hard, you thought the guy is going to be dead when he comes out," Rodriguez said. When Jeter was removed from the game and sent to the hospital, Rodriguez replaced him at shortstop.

The Yankees went on to win—and complete a three-game sweep—in the 13th inning when Miguel Cairo scored on a double by reserve catcher John Flaherty, the 14th and last remaining position player available to manager Joe

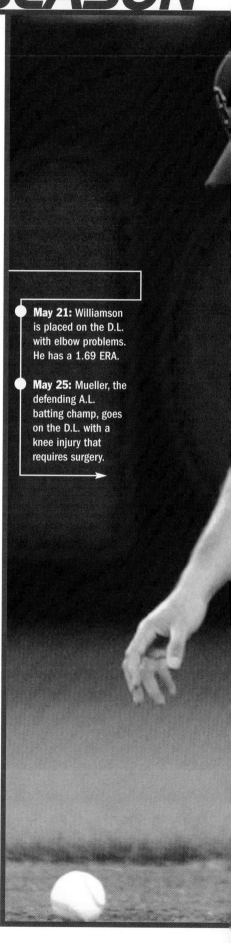

May 21: Williamson is placed on the D.L. with elbow problems. He has a 1.69 ERA.

May 25: Mueller, the defending A.L. batting champ, goes on the D.L. with a knee injury that requires surgery.

A tale of two shortstops: Bloody-faced Derek Jeter is helped off the field after diving into the stands to make an incredible catch in the 12th inning of the series finale. Nomar Garciaparra boots a ground ball, one of two costly errors he made in the opener.

The only bright spot in an 11-3 first-game loss was Johnny Damon's two home runs, both off Javier Vazquez. They were overshadowed by three errors—including one by Kevin Millar (below)—that led to four unearned runs.

Torre.

"When you consider who we were playing," Torre said, "and what took place in the game, it would be hard to top this one."

This series showed just how much had changed since the teams' last meeting in April. The Yankees stood at a major league-best 50-26 after the series, while the Red Sox headed home 8½ games behind—much closer to third place than first. Since the end of April, the Sox had stumbled to a 27-29 mark.

"It was a very difficult loss," Red Sox manager Terry Francona said. "At the same time, I've never been so proud of people in my life. It's awful to lose a game like this. It doesn't help in the win column to be proud of people, but I am."

At least the Sox played well in the series finale, which was not the case in the first two games. The Yankees won those games, 11-3 and 4-2, with the aid of six unearned runs.

The Yankees roughed up Derek Lowe in the series opener, scoring nine runs on nine hits over five innings. Hideki Matsui, who was 11-for-19 against Lowe with 11 RBIs, hit a tiebreaking two-run single in a three-run third that made it 4-2 and sent the Yankees on their way. It came one pitch after Jeter and Rodriguez, running on their own, pulled off a double steal.

"That's just some of the little things

Tim Wakefield (top) pitched well enough to win in the second game, but he was plagued by two errors—one by Nomar Garciaparra on a wild throw and another by first baseman David Ortiz, who atoned for his miscue with his A.L.-leading 21st home run (below).

May 31: The Red Sox and Yankees are in a virtual tie for first in the A.L. East.

May 31: Lowe's ERA reaches its high point at 6.84.

June 9: Garciaparra, making his 2004 debut after missing 57 games, goes 1-for-2 in an 8-1 loss to San Diego.

that help you win games," Jeter said. "You pick your spots."

The Red Sox made three errors and allowed four unearned runs, raising their major league-leading error total to 58. Shortstop Nomar Garciaparra, who had missed the first two series with Achilles' tendinitis, allowed Jeter to reach in the fourth when he failed to handle a two-out grounder for his second error of the game. After Gary Sheffield followed with a three-run homer, the Bronx faithful showed their appreciation by chanting, "Thank you, Nomar!"

The next night, Yankees righthander Jon Lieber and Sox knuckleballer Tim Wakefield locked up in a pitcher's duel for the first six-plus innings. Making his first appearance at Yankee Stadium since serving up the home run to Aaron Boone that decided the 2003 ALCS, Wakefield allowed three hits and two unearned runs while Lieber held the Sox to two runs in six innings.

The game came down to the bullpens. And again Sheffield provided the big hit, concluding a 10-pitch battle against Mike Timlin with an RBI double past third base. "The crowd was so loud, I couldn't hear anything, I couldn't feel anything, I wasn't even thinking about my shoulder," said Sheffield, who was playing with a sore left shoulder. "All I could feel was the adrenaline. I've never played in front of a crowd like this."

Yankees fans were treated to 4 hours and 20 minutes of drama in the finale. Manny Ramirez hit two homers, including one in the 13th off Tanyon Sturtze that gave the Sox a short-lived lead. But the Yankees mounted another come-from-behind rally—their league-leading 30th—in the bottom of the inning. Curtis Leskanic got two outs before Ruben Sierra singled and Cairo, down 0-and-2, doubled to right-center field to score the tying run and set the stage for Flaherty's winner.

"When I crossed home plate, that was the best feeling ever," Cairo said.

The third-game loss could not be blamed on Pedro Martinez, who pitched seven strong innings, or Manny Ramirez, who hit two home runs—one in the sixth (right) and another in the 13th that stood as a potential game-winner until the Yankees scored twice in the bottom of the inning.

June 16: Nixon homers in his 2004 debut after missing 63 games with back and quad injuries.

June 20: Boston is blanked for the first time, thanks to a strong outing from Jason Schmidt in San Francisco.

Garciaparra: Out of step with his team?

Shortstop Nomar Garciaparra's view of Derek Jeter's remarkable catch might have been obstructed from his spot in the Boston dugout. If so, it was by choice. While Jeter was spilling his blood for the Yankees, Garciaparra was resting his tired Achilles' for the Red Sox.

As the game unfolded and the drama of a classic battle intensified, Red Sox players moved up to the top step in the dugout to get closer to the action. All except one, that is.

Garciaparra chose to stand one step down from his teammates. Whether or not he was intentionally distancing himself—as some suspect—no one knew but Garciaparra. But one thing was apparent: The Red Sox shortstop wanted to be left alone in his own little world, one that did not include the team that had employed him for eight-plus seasons.

Garciaparra apparently was still reeling over preseason efforts by the Red Sox to sign shortstop Alex Rodriguez, a deal that reportedly would have led to him being traded. And by the end of July, the obviously unhappy Garciaparra indeed would be gone. The Red Sox traded him to the Cubs in a three-team deal that improved their defense and did not negatively affect the clubhouse mood. Not coincidentally, the Red Sox closed the season by going 42-18, the best mark in the major leagues.

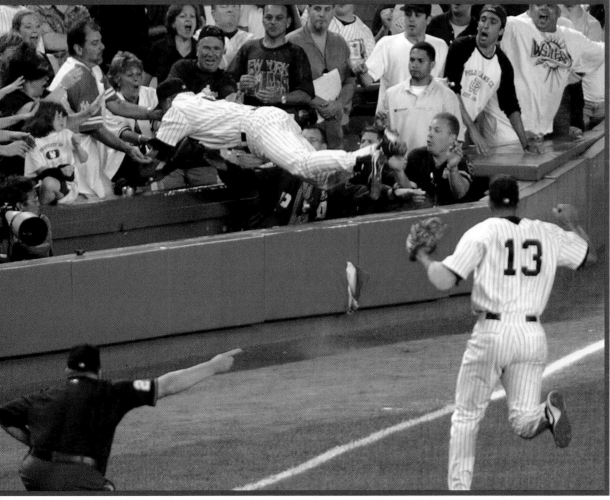

The Yanks made a key play in the 11th inning of the third game when they nailed Gabe Kapler at the plate, and in the 12th when Derek Jeter did his dramatic swan dive into the stands.

Play brawl! Intensity rises in Fenway classic

In baseball's most enduring rivalry, this was a game to remember. Intense action, dramatic comebacks, a walkoff home run. And, oh yes, a benches-clearing brawl that will be seen on highlight clips for years.

The nationally televised Saturday afternoon game, which almost was called off because of an overnight storm, took nearly four hours to complete. In the sixth inning alone, there were 22 batters, 89 pitches thrown and 10 runs scored.

The game wasn't decided until Red Sox third baseman Bill Mueller hit a one-out, two-run homer off Mariano Rivera to cap a three-run ninth inning. The victory ended a four-game Boston losing streak to the Yankees and helped the Sox take the series, 2-1. But the talk in both clubhouses focused on the fight, not the dramatic ending.

The brawl started in the third when Sox starter Bronson Arroyo, his team already trailing 3-0, hit Alex Rodriguez with a pitch on the left arm. As A-Rod, who had driven home the winning run the night before, started toward first, he glared at Arroyo and, according to one report, said, "You don't pull that (bleep) here."

Red Sox catcher Jason Varitek stepped in and told the Yankees third baseman, in not-so-polite terms, to get to first base. As plate umpire Bruce Froemming tried to diffuse the situation, A-Rod appeared to challenge Varitek. The catcher, still wearing his mask, responded with a hard shove to A-Rod's face and the benches and bullpens quickly emptied.

As Rodriguez and Varitek locked up, Yankees starter Tanyon Sturtze grabbed Red Sox outfielder Gabe Kapler from behind. Boston's David Ortiz and Trot Nixon jumped Sturtze and knocked him down, leaving him with a bloody ear and bruised hand.

"I get hit a lot, but I smelled something funny," A-Rod said. "I'm not

A game that included a fight between Red Sox catcher Jason Varitek and Alex Rodriguez ended with a walkoff home run by Bill Mueller (right).

July 13: The A.L., powered by Ortiz and Ramirez homers, wins the All-Star Game and gives Boston home-field advantage in the World Series.

July 16: Foulke picks up his first save since June 13, a sign of the team's inconsistency.

July 17: Ortiz earns a five-game suspension when he is ejected and then nearly hits a couple of umpires when he tosses bats on the field.

going to get into (what Varitek said). But I'll say this: This escalates the rivalry to even a higher level."

Countered Varitek: "He was yelling a few things at Bronson. I told him, in choice words, to get to first base. And then it changed from him yelling at Bronson to yelling at each other, and then things got out of hand."

Varitek, Rodriguez, Kapler and Kenny Lofton were ejected. Sturtze surrendered two runs in the bottom of the inning and left the game because of a finger injury suffered during the brawl. The Yankees took a 3-2 lead into the fourth.

Three innings later, the Yankees delivered what appeared to be a knockout punch by scoring six runs and taking a 9-4 lead. The Sox, however, came back with four in the bottom of the sixth before the Yankees added a run in the seventh to set the stage for Mueller's ninth-inning heroics.

Red Sox manager Terry Francona, who was ejected in the fifth for arguing a call at second base, had to watch the winning hit from his clubhouse office. When Mueller connected on a 3-1 offering, Francona said he "jumped out of my shoes" to join the mob celebrating at the plate. "When I went out on the field, I had no shoes on," Francona said.

The Friday night opener was only slightly less thrilling. The Yankees roughed up Curt Schilling for seven runs on 10 hits in 5⅓ innings to go ahead, 7-4. But the Red Sox, thanks primarily to a three-home run effort by Kevin Millar, fought back to tie the score entering the ninth.

Facing closer Keith Foulke, Yankees right fielder Gary Sheffield doubled off the Green Monster with one out and A-Rod followed with a run-scoring single—what he called his "first big hit as a Yankee." Schilling, head buried in his hands in the dugout, was consoled by pitching coach David Wallace after his worst outing at Fenway Park. The rally took him off the hook and kept him

In the Friday night opener, the Red Sox hit four home runs but still dropped an 8-7 decision to the Yankees. Bill Mueller's two-run homer (above) gave Boston an early lead, and Kevin Millar's eighth-inning blast—his third of the night—gave the Sox a short-lived tie.

July 18: Ramirez misses a second straight game with hamstring problems, raising questions about whether he should have played in the All-Star Game.

July 21: Millar begins a five-game stretch in which he hits six homers and drives in 11 runs.

The Yankees roughed up Curt Schilling for seven runs and 10 hits in 5⅓ innings in his worst outing at Fenway Park.

Alex Rodriguez's "first big hit as a Yankee" drove in Gary Sheffield (right) in the ninth inning and decided the opening game of the series.

undefeated at home, but that was small consolation. When Schilling met with reporters, however, he offered a bright side to the loss—and an unsuspecting hint at what the future would bring.

"It's frustrating," Schilling said, "because we played a game tonight that we should have been playing all year and we haven't been. We were tenacious, we played with intensity, we did all the things we should have been doing. If we play like this every night for the rest of the season, we're going to go to the World Series."

On Sunday night, with presidential candidate John Kerry in attendance, the Red Sox claimed a series victory by beating one of their favorite whipping boys—Jose Contreras, the Cuban defector who would be traded to the White Sox the next week, at least partly because of his struggles against the Red Sox. After giving up eight runs in 5⅓ innings, Contreras' ERA was an unsightly 17.25 at Fenway Park.

The Sox jumped on Contreras for six runs in two innings—Johnny Damon's three-run homer off Pesky's Pole was the big blow—and the lopsided score eased any lingering tension from Saturday's mayhem. Even after Contreras plunked Millar in the back with a curve after he had drilled two long foul balls to left, Millar walked calmly to first and the only person to leave the dugout was Joe Torre. He went out to question the warning issued to his starter, but quickly returned without incident.

Hideki Matsui's grand slam off Mike Timlin brought the Yankees to within three runs in the seventh. But Foulke closed the door on the Yankees—and a memorable weekend—by retiring the last five hitters, insuring a victory that cut the Yankees' A.L. East Division lead over Boston to 7½ games.

It was the final Red Sox-Yankees series for Boston icon Nomar Garciaparra, who was traded to the Cubs later that week. He was 5-for-14 in the series.

Jason Varitek delivers a glove to the face of Alex Rodriguez, touching off a third inning brawl in Game 2. Some say the fight triggered Boston's second-half surge

July 29: Garciaparra gets his final hit and final RBI in his final game in a Red Sox uniform.

July 31: Garciaparra is dealt to the Cubs in a three-way deal that brings Mientkiewicz and Cabrera to Boston. The Sox also acquire Roberts.

August 1: Bellhorn is hit by a pitch that breaks his thumb.

Manny Ramirez celebrates (far left) after Bill Mueller's walkoff home run in the bottom of the ninth decided the wild second game. Mariano Rivera leaves the mound after a rare blown save.

Inspired by their Game 2 win, the Sox blasted three home runs the next day off Jose Contreras (top)—including one by Johnny Damon (left) and another by Kevin Millar, who got a high-five from presidential candidate John Kerry.

Red Sox miss chance to reel in Yankees

When the Red Sox made their final regular-season visit to Yankee Stadium, they were on a roll. Since trading Nomar Garciaparra, they had posted a 32-11 record, and a sweep in the Bronx could have pulled them to within a half game of the Yankees in the A.L. East.

Considering the Red Sox had trailed by 10½ games in mid-August, even the ever-cool Yankees had to be looking over their shoulders. Boston's offense was clicking, its pitching had been steady and its defense was much improved with the addition of shortstop Orlando Cabrera from the Expos and first baseman Doug Mientkiewicz in the Garciaparra deal.

The critical weekend started promising enough for the Red Sox when they stunned Mariano Rivera and a soldout crowd at Yankee Stadium with a two-run, ninth-inning rally that produced a 3-2 victory in the Friday night opener. On a wet field in a game delayed twice by rain—the remnants of Hurricane Ivan—Cabrera singled home the tying run and Johnny Damon hit a single to short center that brought home the winner. The drama intensified with Rivera appearing to question why Kenny Lofton could not catch Damon's looping fly ball.

Trot Nixon had led off the inning with a walk and Kevin Millar was hit by a pitch, setting the stage for Boston's second win over Rivera since the All-Star break—and only his second loss of the season. "You don't get too many opportunities against a guy like him," said outfielder Dave Roberts, who scored the tying run after pinch running for Nixon and stealing second

Pinch runner Dave Roberts gets a congratulatory bump from Kevin Millar after scoring the tying run in Boston's come-from-behind win in the series opener. Johnny Damon gets the game-winning hit (above).

August 9: Schilling loses to Tampa Bay, his only home loss of the season.

August 15: Boston loses to the White Sox and falls 10½ games behind the Yankees.

base. "We find ways to win. We feel confident when we take the field every night."

But the Yankees, as they always do, regrouped in a hurry and outscored the Sox, 25-5, in the next two games to reassert their control of the division. With two weeks left in the season, the Yankees' lead was back to 4½ games and Boston's hopes of winning the division were all but gone.

After their wrenching Friday loss, the Yankees quickly restored order on Saturday. When Alex Rodriguez knocked out Derek Lowe in the second inning by slamming a line drive off the righthander's ankle, the Yankees already had scored five runs in the first and put their leadoff man on in the second. RBI singles by Gary Sheffield, Hideki Matsui and Bernie Williams contributed to four more runs that staked the Yankees to a 9-0 lead. Williams, who had been benched on Friday, had three RBIs after his first three at-bats.

Yankees starter Jon Lieber fared much better than Lowe. He did not allow a hit until two were out in the seventh and the Yankees were on top, 13-0. The crowd was roaring with every out until David Ortiz ended the no-hit bid with a home run to left-center field. Lieber, pitching for a spot in the postseason rotation, walked one and lasted into the ninth to improve his record to 5-1 in games following Yankees losses.

The Yankees' approach for Saturday's game was even more serious than usual. "Jeter was teasing everybody—you guys are serious today," Sheffield said. "There wasn't a whole lot going on in the locker room and it was real quiet, but once we got on the field, the bats started making noise and it was a nice

Left fielder Manny Ramirez reaches over the wall to pull back a home run bid by Yankees second baseman Miguel Cairo in the series opener.

August 16: Boston beats Toronto to start a six-game winning streak and 23-2 run.

August 23: The Red Sox sweep the White Sox—their first road sweep since April 23-25 at Yankee Stadium.

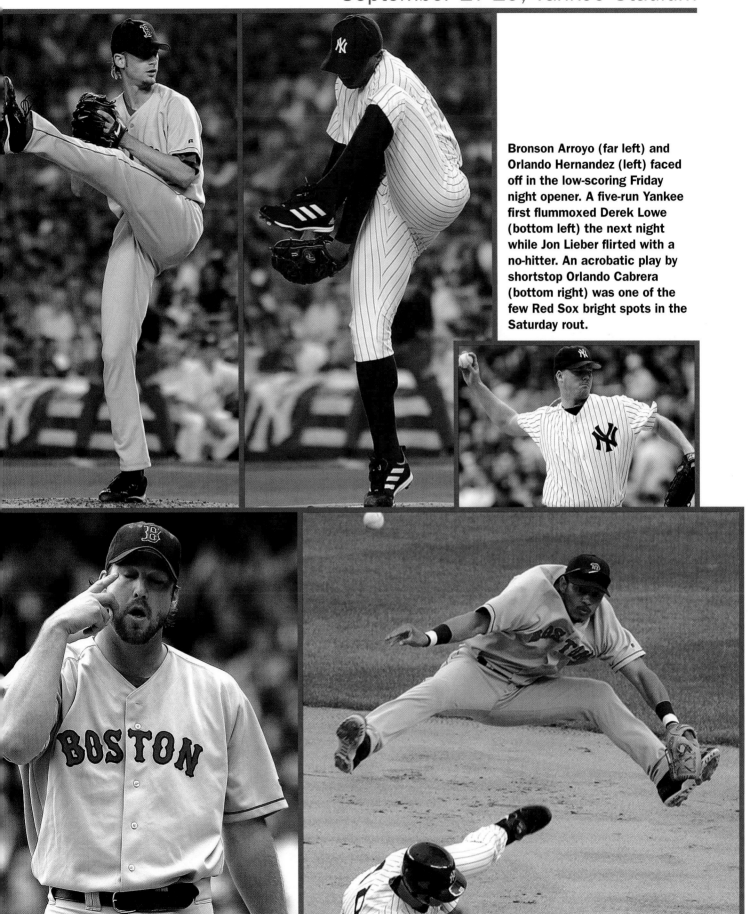

Bronson Arroyo (far left) and Orlando Hernandez (left) faced off in the low-scoring Friday night opener. A five-run Yankee first flummoxed Derek Lowe (bottom left) the next night while Jon Lieber flirted with a no-hitter. An acrobatic play by shortstop Orlando Cabrera (bottom right) was one of the few Red Sox bright spots in the Saturday rout.

sight."

Pedro Martinez, who claims to be the "most hated" man in New York, was silenced in Sunday's series finale. He didn't make it through the sixth as the Yankees cruised to an 11-1 victory. Martinez gave up eight runs and eight hits, including home runs to Derek Jeter, Sheffield and Jorge Posada. "I never felt the ball right today," said Martinez, who did go over the 200-innings mark in a season for the first time in four years.

Another sellout crowd chanted long and loud, "PAAAY-DROH!" when he exited after surrendering Posada's homer in the sixth. It marked the first time since June 2002 that Martinez had lost back-to-back starts. It also was the first time since that same month that he allowed three homers in a game.

Yankees starter Mike Mussina had no problems with the Sox. He improved his career record as a Yankee to 3-2 over Martinez by working seven innings and allowing just one run. The win was Mussina's third in a row after struggling during his return from an elbow injury.

While disappointing, the setback did little to lessen Martinez's confidence in himself and his team. "If we get to the playoffs," Martinez said, "we're not the ones who are going to be afraid."

The Yankees appeared ready for any Boston challenge. "This team doesn't look back, we keep going forward," Sheffield said. "You never see panic in anybody's face. Everyone knows this is what we need to do."

Pedro Martinez, the self-proclaimed 'most hated man in New York,' was shelled for eight runs in the finale, much to the delight of the Yankee Stadium faithful.

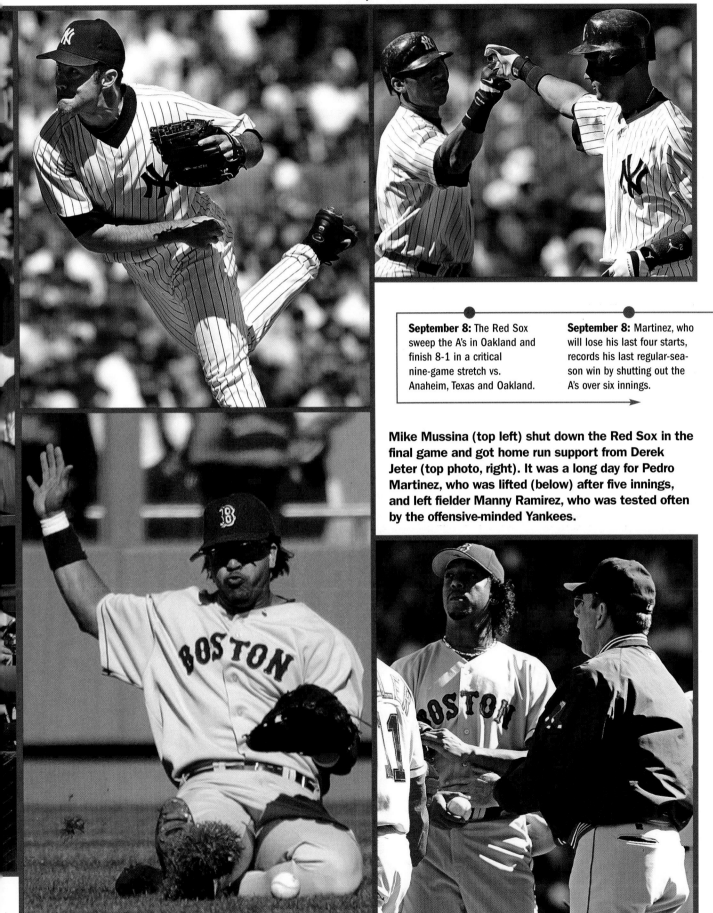

September 8: The Red Sox sweep the A's in Oakland and finish 8-1 in a critical nine-game stretch vs. Anaheim, Texas and Oakland.

September 8: Martinez, who will lose his last four starts, records his last regular-season win by shutting out the A's over six innings.

Mike Mussina (top left) shut down the Red Sox in the final game and got home run support from Derek Jeter (top photo, right). It was a long day for Pedro Martinez, who was lifted (below) after five innings, and left fielder Manny Ramirez, who was tested often by the offensive-minded Yankees.

The little things count as Sox get last laugh

Everything about Red Sox-Yankees is big, which is why pitcher Pedro Martinez created such a stir in the Boston locker room before the second game of the final regular-season series between the bitter rivals. Martinez arrived with fine-worthy lateness, about an hour before the first pitch, accompanied by 28-inch Dominican entertainer Nelson de la Rosa, a k a Mahow Mahow, the Lil' Dancing Man.

Pedro's Mini Me, the "world's smallest actor" and the third smallest man, provided a big relief of tension for Red Sox teammates. The jokes and "little" comments by players were fast and furious. Even Terry Francona looked behind de la Rosa as if to check for batteries.

What really was not funny was that less than 24 hours earlier, critics were thinking *Little* of *Grady* Francona.

The Boston manager had sent Martinez out to pitch the eighth inning of the series opener with Boston ahead 4-3, thanks to a Johnny Damon homer in the bottom of the seventh. Martinez had thrown 101 pitches to get that far, and No. 103 was launched by Hideki Matsui into the Boston bullpen, which is where, based upon recent history, Francona probably should have looked for a pitcher to begin the inning.

In October of 2003, former Boston manager Grady Little had stayed with Martinez in ALCS Game 7 despite a similarly high pitch count, and the Yankees erased a 5-2 Boston lead in the eighth inning. The tragic number for Martinez is 100, a pitch count at which point his ERA balloons from Cy-like to sigh-inducing. After Matsui's tying home run, Francona stayed with Martinez through a double by Bernie Williams, a strikeout, then a go-ahead single by Ruben Sierra.

Martinez never attempted eye contact with Francona when he finally came to the mound. He just dropped the ball in Francona's hand and retreated

A homer by Manny Ramirez helped the Red Sox cause in the series opener, but Pedro Martinez could not hold a lead and fell again to his Yankee 'Daddy.'

September 16: Schilling wins No. 20, although he gives up four earned runs to the Devil Rays.

September 18: Boston rallies for a 3-2 win over Mariano Rivera and the Yankees, pulling to within 2½ games of first.

with disgust to the locker room. The frustration clearly was at an all-time peak for the team's one-time ace during a postgame media session, when Martinez said, "I just tip my cap and call the Yankees my daddy."

The numbers from his starts during recent years against the Yankees provide proof of paternity. The fifth winningest pitcher in franchise history, Martinez went into the Friday start with two wins in 10 previous starts against New York, dating back to August of 2002. Against the rest of baseball, Martinez had a .672 winning percentage over that span.

"You just have to give them credit and say, 'Hey you guys beat me, not my team.' They beat me. And let it go. They're that good. They're that hot right now, at least against me," Martinez said. "I wish they would disappear and never come back."

One thing the 2004 Yankees always seemed to do is come back. They trailed Martinez twice before getting even and then going on top to stay. New York's 6-4 win was their major league-record 59th come-from-behind victory of the season.

Too often, the Yankees say, they have to come back to beat Boston. The reverse is true among Red Sox players. Boston's 12-5 win on Saturday was followed by an 11-4 victory on Sunday as the teams completed a 19-game regular-season slate, the Red Sox winning 11 times. Since the start of the 2003 season, these franchises had played 45 games (regular season and playoffs) that mattered. The win totals: Red Sox 23, Yankees 22.

Too much of a good thing? Not according to television ratings, and therefore broadcasters feeding off the

In addition to his prowess handling knuckleballer Tim Wakefield, catcher Doug Mirabelli contributed with his bat. His double and homer drove in four runs in the second game.

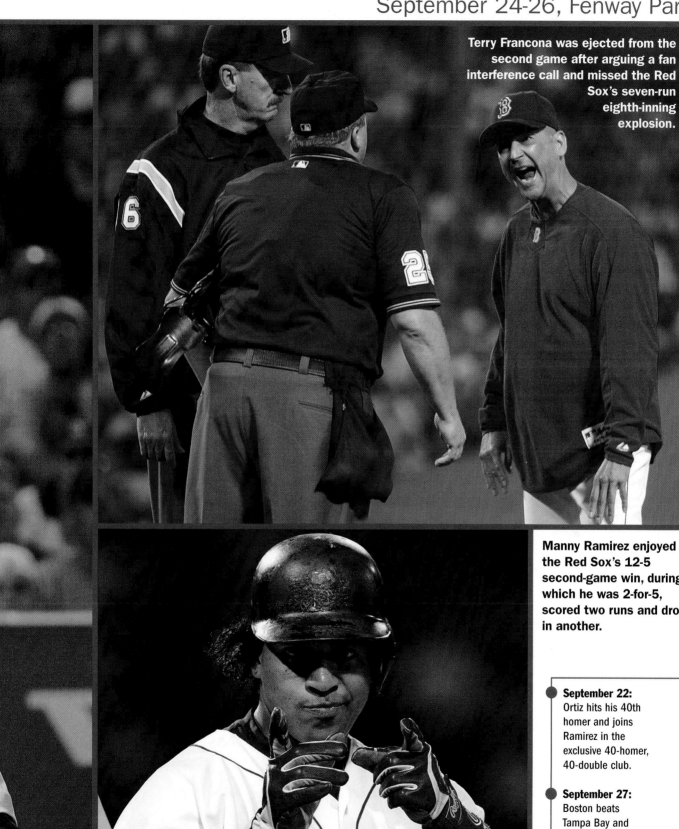

Terry Francona was ejected from the second game after arguing a fan interference call and missed the Red Sox's seven-run eighth-inning explosion.

Manny Ramirez enjoyed the Red Sox's 12-5 second-game win, during which he was 2-for-5, scored two runs and drove in another.

September 22:
Ortiz hits his 40th homer and joins Ramirez in the exclusive 40-homer, 40-double club.

September 27:
Boston beats Tampa Bay and clinches the A.L. wild card.

buzz of contempt—a contempt fertilized by an excess of familiarity. "We probably play them too much," said Damon. "There's too much anxiety brewing."

Besides the frustrating reminder involving a gassed-out Martinez, this three-game set—rendered mostly meaningless in terms of the division race after the Yankees' Friday night win lifted them 5½ games ahead of the Sox with a week left in the season—included managerial ejections for each side, several players tossed, a few bench-clearing stare-offs, many brush-back and behind-the-back pitches, some well-aimed balls to the ribs, two wrapped hands and one well-placed elbow to the back (New York batter Kenny Lofton to Boston first baseman Doug Mientkiewicz).

A typical three-game weekend between these teams. A complete reversal from the previous weekend, when New York lost a stomach-churning game Friday and followed with blowouts on Saturday and Sunday. As the complete reversal paraded to a conclusion with Curt Schilling throwing a one-hitter for seven innings, Boston's down-with-the-crowd ownership group wandered through the bleachers, where chairman Tom Werner barehanded Bill Mueller's 12th home run. Werner appeared in a postgame broadcast with his fielding hand bandaged and said, "It was a tribute to Kevin Brown."

Brown started Sunday for the first time since breaking a bone in his left hand in a locker room fit of anger. Even with the special padding on his glove hand, he lasted only eight batters and two-thirds of an inning.

Alex Rodriguez, who had now participated for an entire year in this rivalry after nearly being acquired by Boston early in the offseason, was introduced to its fury via Jason Varitek's glove to the face a month earlier. When asked Sunday to sum up a year of Red Sox-Yankees, he couldn't because, he said, "This is not over."

October 1: Damon hits his 20th homer to cap a season that also included 123 runs, a .304 average and 94 RBIs.

October 2: Varitek steals his 10th base. He finishes second on the team behind Damon.

Curt Schilling recorded his 21st win in the season finale against the Yankees, during which tempers flared when first baseman Doug Mientkiewicz (13) received a well-placed elbow to the back from runner Kenny Lofton (left).

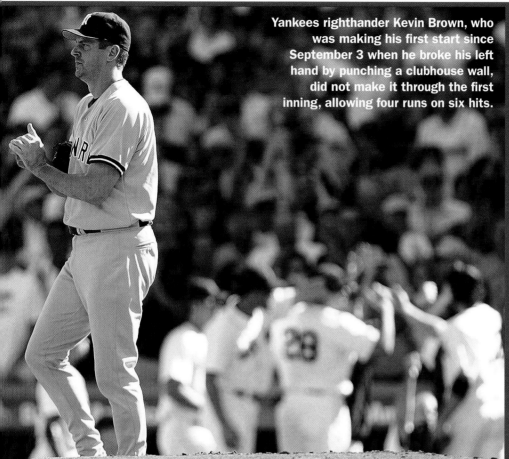

Yankees righthander Kevin Brown, who was making his first start since September 3 when he broke his left hand by punching a clubhouse wall, did not make it through the first inning, allowing four runs on six hits.

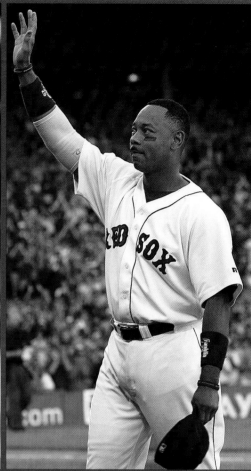

The Fenway crowd gave a touching ovation to Ellis Burks (above) when it was announced he was playing his last regular-season game. The 18-year veteran began his career with Boston. The Red Sox were saluted in similar fashion after the game.

THE SECOND

KEEP THE FAITH
GOD BLESS THE
RED SOX
TEAM THAT WE LOVE
UnWine'd

SEASON

Game 1   RED SOX 9, ANGELS 3

'Real season' begins, and Schilling delivers

Curt Schilling knows as well as anyone: Things are not the same in the postseason. As the righthander says, "assessing your performance takes on a different meaning" in October. In other words, what matters most is who gets the W and who gets the L.

In Game 1, Schilling and the Red Sox got the W, 9-3.

All season, Schilling has met the great expectations that go with being a hired gun for a franchise that hasn't won a World Series since 1918. He won a major league-best 21 games and finished second in the A.L. with a 3.26 ERA and third with 226⅔ innings pitched. In an era in which overhyping is the norm, Schilling delivered. But that was the regular season, which in places like New York and Boston is nothing more than a 162-game prelim for the real season.

Schillling didn't pitch great against the Angels, but he was good enough. Sometimes his mere presence is enough. The offense can relax a little when Schilling pitches. Teammates trust he will keep them in the game. In this one, he held the Angels scoreless until the offense took control during a seven-run fourth inning.

Schilling lasted 6⅔ innings and allowed nine hits and two earned runs. He said his velocity was great but his command wasn't. Attribute part of his success to shutting down Vladimir Guerrero, the slugger who had put the Angels on his back for the final week of the season and led them to the A.L. West title. In his last six regular-season games, Guerrero had gone 15-for-24 with six homers and 11 RBIs.

But in his first postseason game, Guerrero was hitless and stranded

				R	H	E
BOSTON	100	700	010	9	11	1
ANAHEIM	000	100	200	3	9	1

W: SCHILLING (1-0, 2.70)   L: WASHBURN (0-1, 8.10)

Curt Schilling clearly was the focus of the Red Sox's Game 1 win, but Kevin Millar (above) also had his moment in the spotlight when he homered in a seven-run fourth-inning explosion.

three runners. He swung at the first pitch in four of his five at-bats and didn't take one until his fourth at-bat. The notoriously aggressive Guerrero swung at five pitches outside the strike zone.

With the Red Sox up 1-0, two on and one out in the Angels' third, Schilling got Guerrero to fly out to right and Garret Anderson to ground out. The game took a dramatic turn in the fourth when the Red Sox knocked out Angels starter Jarrod Washburn and broke open the game.

Kevin Millar's two-run homer started the scoring, and Manny Ramirez's three-run blast finished it. In between was a costly throwing error by third baseman Chone Figgins. With the bases loaded, Figgins fielded a grounder and had what appeared to be a sure force at the plate. But his throw sailed away from catcher Bengie Molina, and two runs scored.

By the time they were done, the Red Sox had their biggest inning in postseason history and Schilling had what he was expected to have—a postseason victory. And the Angels had a hole to climb out of.

David Ortiz (above), Manny Ramirez (top) and Johnny Damon scored five runs and combined for five Game 1 hits.

Manny Ramirez, who hit a three-run homer, gets a hug from Gabe Kapler as Johnny Damon looks on. Curt Schilling (left) received first-rate defensive help from shortstop Orlando Cabrera (top right) and first baseman Kevin Millar (above). Millar also contributed two hits, a home run and two RBIs.

Game 2

RED SOX 8, ANGELS 3

With Pedro in form, Sox go two games up

After the Red Sox's Game 1 victory, Johnny Damon joked that this year's club had undergone a transformation. Last year's "Cowboys" have become this year's "Idiots," he said, a silly reference to all the zany personalities on the roster—each of whom comes with his own unique hairstyle. From Damon's shoulder-length locks and Manny Ramirez's bushy curls to Kevin Millar's ever-changing coiffures, the Red Sox could be mistaken for a collection of deadbeats with baggy pants and broad shoulders.

But don't let looks deceive you. This is one solid team, as it proved again in Game 2 by beating Anaheim at Angel Stadium.

The game was much closer than the final score indicates. It was 3-1 Angels after five, 3-3 after six and 4-3 Red Sox entering the ninth. Neither starting pitcher, Pedro Martinez nor Bartolo

Colon, was dominant, but both were pretty darn good. Martinez allowed three runs in seven innings and eased the worries of a Red Sox Nation not sure what to think after seeing him close the season with four losses while allowing 21 runs in $23\frac{1}{3}$ innings. Against the Angels, Martinez's fastball was touching 93-94 mph a week after he struggled to reach 90. Colon had to battle to hold the Red Sox to three runs and seven hits over six innings. He worked out of bases-loaded jams in each of the first two innings, allowing only one run but throwing 55 pitches.

Colon clearly tired in the sixth when he gave up a two-run homer to catcher Jason Varitek, who had looked bad striking out in his first two at-bats. After Millar singled with two out, Varitek hit Colon's 110th pitch over the right-center field wall. The Angels, who had taken a 3-1 lead in the fifth on Vladimir

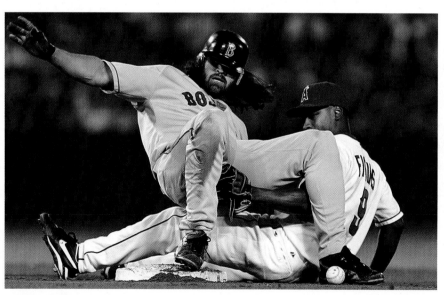

The Red Sox, down 3-1, reeled in the Angels in the sixth inning when Jason Varitek hit a two-run homer and received a warm greeting (right) from David Ortiz. Johnny Damon set up the go-ahead run an inning later when he stole second, knocking the ball loose from Anaheim's Chone Figgins.

Guerrero's two-run single, had been caught. "It was right in his wheelhouse," Colon said.

An inning later, the Red Sox pushed across the go-ahead run against Angels relief ace Francisco Rodriguez. The Sox made the most of an infield hit by Bill Mueller, a wild pitch by Colon (that should have been handled by Jose Molina), a walk to Mark Bellhorn and Manny Ramirez's sacrifice fly—the only ball to leave the infield.

The Red Sox got breathing room in the ninth when they scored four runs off Brendan Donnelly, three on a double by shortstop Orlando Cabrera.

Back in New England, fans who had stayed up late for a night game on the West Coast finally were able to go to bed smiling. Their Sox were up 2-0 with the next two games scheduled for Fenway Park, where the team posted a 55-26 record in the regular season. Just as comforting was the belief that the sometimes mysterious Pedro was pitching like the old marvelous Pedro.

As Damon told reporters while packing for the flight home, "Going back 2-0 with a day off, you can't ask for much better than that."

Pedro Martinez (above) points skyward after striking out Chone Figgins to end the seventh inning. Martinez had six strikeouts and a fastball clocked in the low 90s. Manny Ramirez gets a high five from Doug Mientkiewicz after scoring one of the Red Sox's four ninth-inning runs.

Kevin Millar signals the obvious as the Red Sox score four ninth-inning runs, one by Jason Varitek (top) on Orlando Cabrera's bases-loaded double. Third baseman Bill Mueller tags out and hurdles Jeff DaVanon, who was trying to advance in the third inning on a hit by Angels catcher Jose Molina.

Game 3 RED SOX 8, ANGELS 6

Ortiz's Monster shot sweeps away Angels

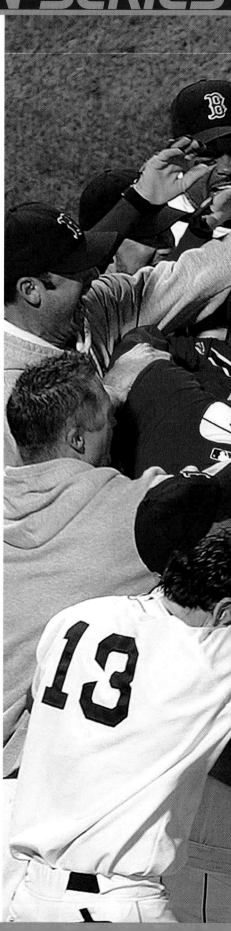

Well, maybe this really would be their year. Judging by David Ortiz's heroics on the field and the Red Sox's celebration in their Fenway Park clubhouse, this certainly was their day. Ortiz, the cuddly-bear DH, completed the Red Sox's Division Series sweep of the Angels with a two-out, walkoff home run in the 10th inning.

With righthanded closer Troy Percival available, Angels manager Mike Scioscia instead summoned Game 1 starter Jarrod Washburn, a lefty, to face the lefthanded-hitting Ortiz with the score tied 6-6. Washburn hung a slider on his first pitch, and Ortiz, 6-for-11 in the series, hit an opposite-field shot into the seats atop the Green Monster, sending Red Sox Nation into party mode.

As soon as ball met bat, the celebration was on. Said Sox manager Terry Francona: "I looked at (Kevin) Millar, and I said, 'Can he hit a home run here?' It wasn't that far out of my mouth … when it left his bat, our players knew it was gone."

The Angels, trailing 6-1, had tied the game in the seventh with their own brand of dramatics. MVP candidate Vladimir Guerrero did the honors by blasting a grand slam off Red Sox reliever Mike Timlin. Red Sox starter Bronson Arroyo was sharp for six innings, but he tired in the seventh, and the Angels rallied behind three walks, a David Eckstein single and Guerrero's second—and biggest—hit of the series.

Angels starter Kelvim Escobar had put his team in a deep hole by giving up five runs in 3⅓ innings. Five walks and two errors hurt the righthander and put the Angels on the verge of complete embarrassment. But Guerrero's big

Bronson Arroyo (above) allowed three hits over six innings but watched his 6-2 lead disappear in the seventh on a grand slam by Vladimir Guerrero. David Ortiz's walkoff homer in the 10th triggered a wild celebration.

blast changed that, and the Angels even had a chance to take the lead in the ninth when they loaded the bases with one out. But closer Keith Foulke struck out Garret Anderson, the Angels cleanup hitter who finished 2-for-13 in the series, and Troy Glaus.

After tying the game, the Angels turned to their A.L.-best bullpen. Brendan Donnelly finished 2⅓ innings of perfect relief with a 1-2-3 seventh, and Francisco Rodriguez held the Red Sox in check over the eighth and ninth. Johnny Damon led off the 10th with a single, but Rodriguez forced him at second on Mark Bellhorn's bunt. After Rodriguez struck out Manny Ramirez, running his pitch count to 38, Scioscia went out to talk to his ace reliever. Rodriguez indicated he was done.

So were the Angels, as it turned out. The Sox were alive and well—the first team to clinch a spot in a League Championship Series. Afterward, Ramirez, who finished 5-for-13 with seven RBIs, and life-of-the-party Millar sprayed fans with champagne on a victory lap around Fenway. A fitting end to a great day and—who knows?—just maybe a preview of celebrations still to come.

David Ortiz swings and the dugout empties, signaling a 10th-inning conclusion to the Red Sox's ALDS sweep of Anaheim. Ortiz batted .545 in the series, collecting six hits, scoring four runs and driving in four.

Kevin Millar (below left) and Manny Ramirez (below right) had fun at the expense of Angels starter Kelvim Escobar early, but Vladimir Guerrero (27) had a grand old time when he connected in the seventh inning.

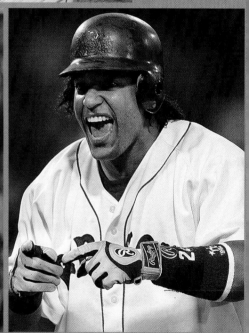

Glad hands and champagne are shared by fan-friendly Kevin Millar and Manny Ramirez (left) and Curt Schilling.

Game 1 — YANKEES 10, RED SOX 7

Schilling gets rocked in tough opening act

Three hundred and sixty days had passed since Aaron Boone's 11th-inning home run ended a classic American League Championship Series between the Red Sox and Yankees. Based on the highlights of the Game 1 rematch in 2004, the wait was worthwhile:

■ Yankees starter Mike Mussina, his knuckle curve baffling the Red Sox, flirted with a perfect game by retiring the first 19 batters.

■ With Mussina dominating on the mound, the Yankees' offense ran up an 8-0 lead in six innings. Left fielder Hideki Matsui, who managed three hits, tied an ALCS record with five RBIs.

■ Down but not out, here came the Red Sox—just when it looked like their victory hopes had been dashed. They scored five runs on five hits in the seventh and came within an eyelash of tying the game in the eighth. Yankees closer Mariano Rivera, who began the day in his home country of Panama to attend a family funeral, arrived at Yankee Stadium after the game was underway and ended it on the mound in a close-call Yankees' victory.

Ho hum! Just another game in American sport's greatest rivalry. "All of those people who say you sit in that dugout and it's so calm, you didn't want to be there tonight," Yankees manager Joe Torre said. "Each game is going to be an emotional roller coaster, there's no question."

The storyline that figured to have the biggest impact was the performance of Sox starter Curt Schilling. The big righthander, who was obtained in the offseason primarily to beat the Yankees in the postseason, sounded up to the task before the game. "I'm not sure I can think of any

Bank of Ame

						L: SCHILLING (0-1, 18.00)	W: MUSSINA (1-0, 5.40)
BOSTON	000	000	520	7	0		
NEW YORK	204	002	02X	10	0		

It was that kind of a night for Sox starter Curt Schilling (opposite), who was pounded by the Yankees and then heard it from gloating fans who reminded him of his pregame comments. One of those big Yankee bats was swung by Hideki Matsui, who drove in an ALCS record-tying five runs.

scenario more enjoyable than making 55,000 people from New York shut up," he said.

Schilling had done just that in the 2001 World Series when he allowed only four runs in 21⅓ innings and his Diamondbacks beat the Yankees in seven games. On this clear, crisp night in the Bronx, however, he was far from 2001 form.

Schilling had trouble keeping his pitches down and the Yankees took quick advantage, scoring six runs before he retired eight batters. He was pitching on a right ankle that required pain shots much of the season, but they didn't help on this Tuesday night. Schilling did not look like the pitcher who won a league-best 21 games in the regular season. His fastball, normally around 95 mph, seldom touched 93. His normally nasty splitter was not sharp and neither was his usually impeccable command. The Red Sox trailed, 6-0, when Schilling was lifted after working a season-low three innings.

Matsui did most of the damage. In the first, he reached down and poked a split-finger fastball into left for a run-scoring double. In the third, he delivered a bases-loaded double. Matsui added an RBI single in the sixth off Tim Wakefield.

Still, Mussina was the man of the hour—the first two hours, anyway. He entered the game having held Red Sox hitters to a .204 average in his four seasons as a Yankee, and he was at his best this night. He was, in fact, perfect until Mark Bellhorn doubled with one out in the seventh. But before Mussina knew what had hit him, David Ortiz singled, Kevin Millar doubled home two runs and Trot Nixon singled home another, forcing a pitching change. Reliever Tanyon Sturtze was greeted by Jason Varitek's two-run homer, cutting the Yankees' once-safe lead to 8-5.

That almost evaporated in the eighth when reliever Tom Gordon allowed two singles and a heart-stopping blast by

Grimacing and head-scratching were the order of the day for Curt Schilling, who lasted only three innings and watched the Red Sox fall into a first-game hole from which they could not escape.

Yankees starter Mike Mussina (below) kept Red Sox hitters (from left) Manny Ramirez, David Ortiz and Kevin Millar frustrated and hitless through six innings. Johnny Damon finished with four strikeouts.

David Ortiz that bounced high off the left-center field wall—a two-run triple that brought the Sox to within 8-7.

Torre called on the reliable Rivera, even though his closer was emotionally and physically drained from his long, hard day. Rivera stranded Ortiz at third by getting Millar to pop out. After the Yankees reclaimed a three-run cushion in the bottom of the inning on Bernie Williams' two-run double, Rivera allowed two ninth-inning singles but ended the game by inducing Bill Mueller to ground into a double play.

"It was tough, leaving my family," Rivera said. "I came here and my friends, my teammates treated me like a king, and that was something special and I appreciate that. It helped me bigtime."

From near-perfect to near-disaster, fortune did a quick about-face for Mike Mussina in the seventh inning. After Mark Bellhorn's double ended his no-hit bid (top), the Red Sox scored five runs in the inning—two on a home run by Jason Varitek off Mussina's replacement, Tanyon Sturtze.

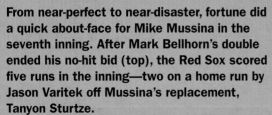

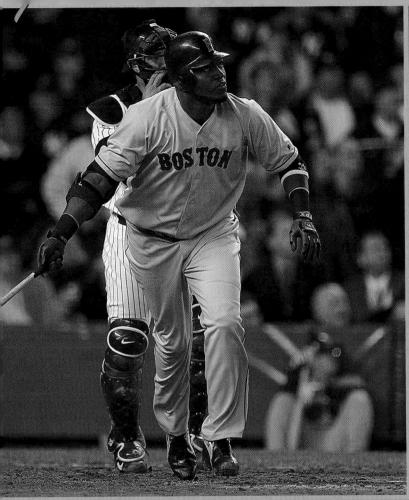

David Ortiz came within a foot or so of tying the game in the eighth inning when Yankees left fielder Hideki Matsui couldn't quite reach his booming triple (above), a drive that bounced off the wall and cut the Red Sox deficit to one.

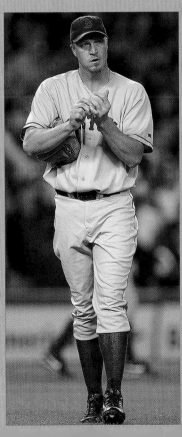

After Mike Timlin (right) surrendered a game-sealing two-run double to Bernie Williams in the bottom of the eighth (above), Mariano Rivera finished the game and earned another save.

Game 2 — YANKEES 3, RED SOX 1

Down 0-2, Sox get bad news about Schilling

On a team packed with All-Stars, a couple of ordinary Johns made the difference as the Yankees took control of the ALCS with a Game 2 victory at Yankee Stadium.

The difference-makers were starting pitcher Jon Lieber and first baseman John Olerud, hardly the first players who come to mind when one thinks of the Yankees. But they were "Johnny-be-very-goods" on this cool autumn evening in the Bronx.

Lieber, who missed all of last season while recovering from elbow surgery, shut down the Red Sox's potent lineup. He pitched seven innings, allowing only one run and three hits while striking out three. Lieber's game plan was to pound strikes and stay ahead of the hitters—a plan he followed to near perfection. He walked only one of the

24 batters he faced and finished with 82 pitches, 57 of them strikes.

Olerud provided the big blow—a two-run, two-strike, one-out homer off Pedro Martinez in the sixth inning that gave the Yankees a welcome 3-0 cushion. It was a great moment for the slick-fielding first baseman who was cast off by the last-place Mariners in August. "I would say it ranks right up there (with the biggest hits in his career)," Olerud said. "It's definitely the freshest in my mind."

For the suddenly staggering Red Sox, an off-the-field development was just as disheartening as their two-games-to-none deficit in the best-of-seven series. Curt Schilling,

Jon Lieber shut down the Red Sox's big bats and John Olerud (inset) delivered a two-strike, two-run, sixth-inning homer off Pedro Martinez that provided the margin of victory.

NEW YORK 100 002 00X | 3 7 0 W: LIEBER (1-0, 1.29)

The Red Sox faced two emotional hurdles before Game 2. The report of Curt Schilling's ankle problem by Dr. Bill Morgan (left) and G.M. Theo Epstein only added to the specter of Pedro Martinez's first return to Yankee Stadium since his 'daddy' quote.

Martinez: 6.0 IP, 4 H, 3 R, 4.50 ERA

the 21-game winner who was acquired to beat the Yankees, was diagnosed with a tendon tear in his ankle, the result of a play he made against the Angels in the A.L. Division Series. With their ace's status uncertain for the remainder of the series, Curse of the Bambino talk was only a matter of time for Red Sox fans.

Martinez, who was serenaded throughout his six innings with chants of "Who's your Daddy," a reference to a comment he made after being pounded by the Yankees in a September game, pitched almost as well as Lieber, at least through 5⅓ innings. He gave up a run in the first on a walk to Derek Jeter and a run-scoring single by Gary Sheffield but stayed out of trouble until the sixth when Olerud hit his home run.

"It was a fastball, but I wanted it away," Martinez said, indicating the pitch had cut back over the plate. "I didn't release it well. And he took full advantage of it."

For the second straight night, the Red Sox did nothing offensively until the late innings. Over the first six innings of the two ALCS games, they had managed only one hit in 37

Ignoring the jeering taunts from Yankee fans, Pedro Martinez pitched six solid innings and struck out seven in a losing cause. Martinez (right) drops to his knees to avoid a throw by catcher Jason Varitek.

72

Derek Jeter provided an early spark for the Yankee[s] he worked Pedro Martinez for a first-inning walk, s[...] second base and scored on Gary Sheffield's single[...]

Yankees fans had fun at the expense of Johnny Damon (above), who struggled to reach base (0-for-8) in the first two games. Starter Jon Lieber also made quick work of Red Sox sluggers Manny Ramirez (far left) and David Ortiz, who were 2-for-7 combined.

at-bats—a harmless third-inning Game 2 single by Orlando Cabrera off Lieber. Cabrera was the only Sox baserunner to reach third in the first seven innings. Johnny Damon, hitless after two games, gave Lieber his biggest challenge in the sixth when he stretched him out in a 16-pitch at-bat that ended with a line drive to Bernie Williams in center.

"That (at-bat) was definitely one of the keys to this game," Yankees manager Joe Torre said. "Because they are trying any way (they can) to get on, make things happen. It all starts with Johnny at the top of that lineup. He makes a lot of things happen."

Damon was not the only Red Sox player struggling at the plate. Mark Bellhorn, Kevin Millar and Bill Mueller had one hit each after the first two games. As a team, the Sox were hitting .224.

"I don't think we've swung the bat very effectively, that's for sure, especially against the two starters," Sox manager Terry Francona said. "We've had no baserunners through the first six innings of either game. I don't think that's being uptight; it's not being very effective."

The Red Sox finally got on the board in the eighth when Trot Nixon singled to lead off the inning, ending Lieber's night. After Lieber ran off the field, as is his custom, to a standing ovation, Jason Varitek greeted Tom Gordon with a double that scored Nixon. Gordon retired Cabrera and Mueller before Torre called on his security blanket, closer Mariano Rivera, to get four outs for the second straight night. Rivera gave up a one-out double to Manny Ramirez in the ninth, but he struck out Ortiz and Millar and sent the Sox home in a big hole.

A hole they might not have their ace to help them dig out of.

The Red Sox managed only three hits off Jon Lieber in seven-plus innings, a frustration that was expressed well by David Ortiz. Boston's only run scored after Lieber was pulled (inset) in the eighth.

The only Red Sox run came in the eighth inning on a fielder's choice grounder by Orlando Cabrera (left). Mariano Rivera took care of the ninth in typical fashion and the Yankees celebrated another win, led by Derek Jeter and Alex Rodriguez (inset).

Game 3 YANKEES 19, RED SOX 8

Bombs away: Fenway rout has Sox reeling

The Yankees are famous for taking their game to another level in October, but this was an amazing performance, even by their lofty standards. Just check the numbers: 19 runs, the most in Yankees' postseason history, 22 hits, four homers and eight doubles. This franchise really knows how to spoil a night—make that an entire season—for the Red Sox and their fans.

By the end of the 4-hour, 20-minute marathon—the longest nine-inning postseason game ever played—the Yankees had blown away the Sox and moved to within one victory of their 40th American League pennant. The setback left the Red Sox one loss away from extending their World Series futility to 86 years. Judging by the glum looks on faces of the Fenway faithful, this was as disheartening as any Sox setback in recent memory.

"You can't expect to go in against the Red Sox and do what we did tonight," Yankees manager Joe Torre said. "We knew going in that it was going to be a tough series. And it's not over yet because they are certainly capable of winning ballgames. But to be up 3-0, yeah, I think we're surprised by the fact that we've done that."

"It was disappointing for everybody, but we're not done," Red Sox manager Terry Francona said.

From the first inning,

when the Yankees scored on Alex Rodriguez's double and Hideki Matsui's two-run homer, it was increasingly apparent pitchers were in for a long night. Even the Red Sox, who had not scored in the first six innings of the first two games, got busy early with four runs in the second and two more in the third. The Sox even enjoyed their first lead of the series—4-3 after two innings—but it was gone before they batted in the third.

The Yankees really got serious in the fourth when they scored five runs off three Red Sox pitchers. Gary Sheffield hit a three-run homer and Ruben Sierra a two-run double to give New York an 11-6 lead. Rodriguez and Sheffield added run-scoring doubles in the fifth and, after a 1-2-3 sixth, the Yankees struck for another four runs to go up 17-6. They finished their rampage in the

The scoreboard tells a sad story for Red Sox fans and Manny Ramirez, who watched Yankees left fielder Hideki Matsui (above) drive in five runs.

BOSTON 042 000 200 | 8 15 0 L: MENDOZA (0-1, 4.50)

ninth when Matsui hit his second two-run homer.

Every Yankee starter had at least one hit except first baseman John Olerud, who left early with a foot injury. The most damage was done by Rodriguez, Sheffield and Matsui, who were a combined 12-for-16 with 13 runs and 12 RBIs. Matsui and Rodriguez set an LCS record by scoring five runs apiece, and Bernie Williams, who had four hits and three RBIs, set career LCS records for hits, RBIs and total bases. But it was Matsui, who enjoyed his second five-RBI game of the series, that had Torre talking.

"He's ice cold," Torre said of his Japanese slugger. "He's cool under pressure, and I think that's probably the most important ingredient. We all know he's talented, we all know he's strong. He never gives away an at-bat. Evidence, we have this big lead and he has a two-run home run his last time up. But knock on wood, he's huge hitting for us in the cleanup spot."

Six Sox pitchers tried to slow the barrage, but none had much luck. Starter Bronson Arroyo allowed six runs and six hits and did not retire a batter in the third before he was pulled. Knuckleballer Tim Wakefield, who was scheduled to start the next night, got 10 outs, more than any other Boston pitcher, but also gave up five runs.

"We had a night tonight where none of our pitchers located, none of them," said Francona in the understatement of the night.

The Red Sox could take small consolation in their offense, which came alive with 15 hits. Yankees starter Kevin Brown could not make it through the third, and his departure allowed Javier Vazquez an opportunity. Vazquez responded with $4\frac{1}{3}$ innings and a victory, even though he gave up four runs on seven hits.

On a night that belonged to the big bats, that was about as good as any pitcher could expect.

Boston DH David Ortiz and Yankee Ruben Sierra shared a pregame laugh, but Ortiz's smile faded when the big bats started booming. Joe Torre (below, 6) got lots of mileage out of his top three hitters—Derek Jeter (2), Alex Rodriguez (right) and Gary Sheffield, who combined to score 10 of the team's 19 runs.

After Terry Francona pulled Bronson Arroyo, he handed the ball to five relievers, including (from below left) Curtis Leskanic, Tim Wakefield and Alan Embree. But none could stop the Yankees or Hideki Matsui, who finished 5-for-6.

A two-run homer by Trot Nixon (above) helped the Red Sox pull ahead briefly in the second, but that was hardly a concern for Alex Rodriguez and Derek Jeter (top right) on this night. If not for two double plays, the Yankee run total might have been even higher.

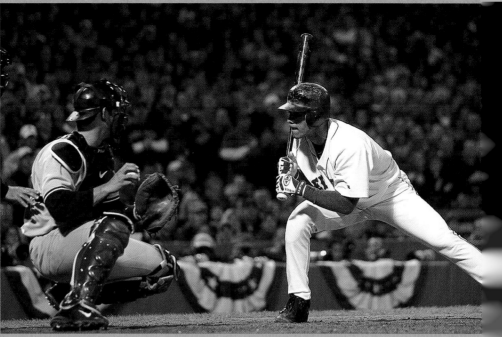

Orlando Cabrera (top right) was a bright spot—going 3-for-4 with two RBIs. The Yankees' huge offensive numbers were enough to scare the most avid Red Sox fans—including author Stephen King (top left). The Fenway Park nightmare was especially tough to watch for Red Sox players.

Game 4 RED SOX 6, YANKEES 4

12th-inning home run keeps Sox breathing

Three outs away from an embarrassing ALCS sweep and facing an uphill climb that no major league team had ever accomplished, the Red Sox gave their shellshocked fans a rally to remember and hope for more in the days ahead. First they tied Game 4 with a ninth-inning run off Yankees closer Mariano Rivera, and then they kept their World Series dream alive when David Ortiz drove a 12th-inning pitch from Paul Quantrill into the right field bullpen, a blow that turned tense, frigid Fenway Park into a warm, fan-crazed frenzy.

Ortiz's walkoff two-run shot ended the most dramatic game of what had been a Yankees' runaway series and rekindled, temporarily at least, the fire in the game's hottest rivalry. The blow was made possible by Bill Mueller's game-tying single off Mariano Rivera in the ninth and the six one-run innings of five Red Sox relievers, several of whom had been pounded by Yankee hitters in the previous day's 19-8 loss.

"We are 3-1 now," Ortiz said after he was mobbed by teammates at the plate. "You never know what can happen, but we're going to keep playing the game."

Things had looked bleak entering the ninth when Rivera, working his second inning, walked leadoff man Kevin Millar and then watched pinch runner Dave Roberts steal second. That set the stage for Mueller, who shot a grounder up the middle that tied the game, prompting Rivera to swing his arm in disgust over his first blown LCS save and only the fourth in 36 postseason chances. Rivera avoided further damage when he overcame an error and got Ortiz on a fly ball to right with the bases loaded.

"Having a one-run lead in the ninth

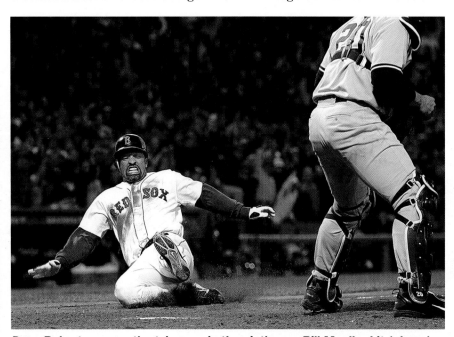

Dave Roberts scores the tying run in the ninth on a Bill Mueller hit (above), setting the stage for David Ortiz's second walkoff homer of the postseason. After Ortiz's 12th-inning blow, pandemonium erupted at Fenway.

BOSTON   000 030 001 002 | 6 8 0   W: LESKANIC (1-0, 10.13)

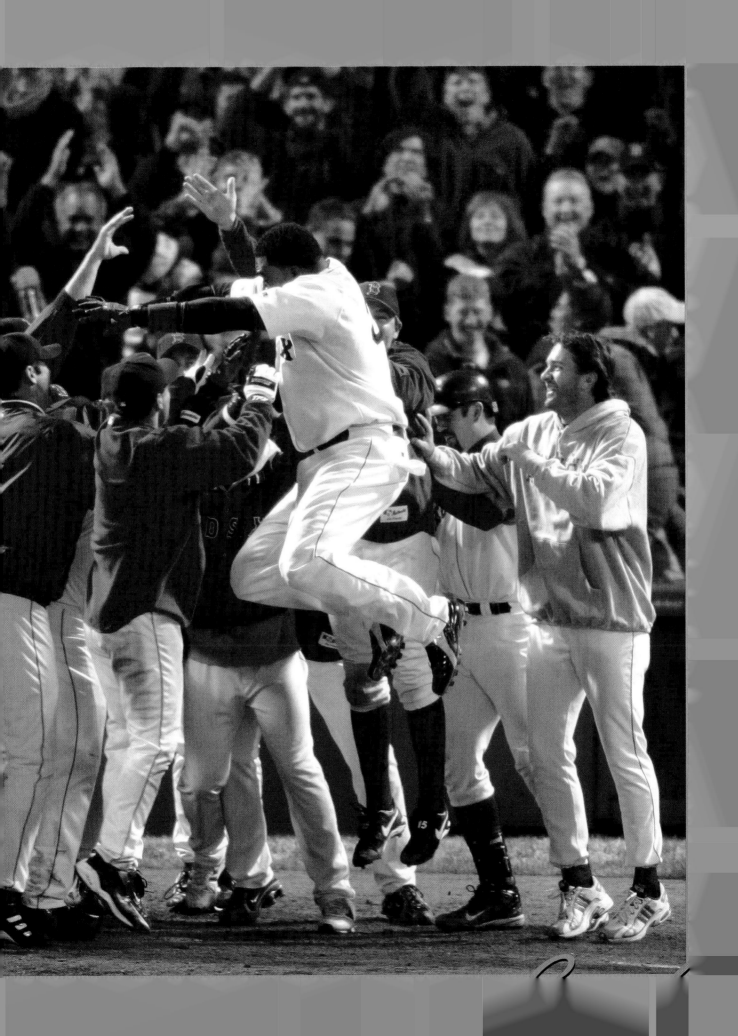

inning, it certainly is disappointing," Yankees manager Joe Torre said. "We're so used to Mo going out there and getting people out. It's just that the walk and the stolen base were the difference in that ninth inning. But you have to come back."

The Yankees threatened in the 11th when they loaded the bases with two out for Bernie Williams. But Curtis Leskanic, who had been rocked in Game 3, retired Williams on a soft fly to Johnny Damon in center field. Leskanic also stranded a runner at second in the 12th by striking out Miguel Cairo.

"Their bullpen did a great job. They made pitches when they had to," Yankees shortstop Derek Jeter said. "We definitely let opportunities get by. We know they're not going to give up. But we're exactly in the position we want to be in."

The Yankees, who stranded 14 runners, had taken the early lead on Alex Rodriguez's two-run homer in the third. That held through the fourth, thanks to Orlando Hernandez, the Yankees' top starter after the All-Star break who was making his first start of the postseason because of an ailing right arm. Hernandez was his own worst

Ortiz: 2-for-5, HR, 4 RBIs

Surprise starter Derek Lowe (above) surrendered a third-inning homer to Alex Rodriguez (far right), but otherwise pitched well. Good defense also helped, particularly a second-inning play on which Sox catcher Jason Varitek tagged out Hideki Matsui at the plate.

Before David Ortiz took center stage with his walkoff homer, he delivered a two-run, fifth-inning single that scored Johnny Damon (left) and Orlando Cabrera (center). Jason Varitek (33) gives his teammates a welcome-home salute.

Down by one in the ninth inning with Mariano Rivera warming up in the Yankees bullpen, things looked bleak for Cabrera and the Fenway faithful.

enemy in the fifth, issuing three walks, an RBI single to shortstop Orlando Cabrera and a two-run single to Ortiz that gave the Red Sox a brief 3-2 lead.

Sox starter Derek Lowe, who was inserted into the rotation only because of Curt Schilling's ankle injury, kept pace with Hernandez before leaving in the sixth. Lowe, who gave up three runs and six hits in 5⅓ innings, was relieved by Mike Timlin in the Yankees' two-run sixth.

The 5-hour, 2-minute game, which came on the heels of a 4-hour, 20-minute Game 3 marathon, ended at 1:22 a.m., but that didn't stop an enthusiastic celebration from spilling onto Yawkey Way. No team in baseball history had ever come back to win a best-of-seven postseason series after losing the first three games, a note that was lost in the Fenway frenzy. The late night left both teams with the prospect of having to play Game 5 in about 15 hours.

The game marked the third time the Yankees and Red Sox had gone to extra innings in the postseason—and all three were decided by a walkoff homer.

Three outs away from being swept, the Sox survived when Bill Mueller's ninth-inning single drove in an ecstatic Dave Roberts (right) with the tying run.

The Dave Roberts-Kevin Millar ninth-inning chest-bump celebration (above left) was nothing compared to the one that started three innings later when Manny Ramirez danced home (above) with the winning run after David Ortiz had sent Fenway Park into a frenzy with his dramatic home run.

Game 5

RED SOX 5, YANKEES 4

'Groundhog Day': Sox win another marathon

One thing was agonizingly clear. In Games 3, 4 and 5 of the A.L. Championship Series, the Red Sox and Yankees were conspiring to see just how long an intensely waged, pressure-packed, absolutely stunning baseball game could last.

The fifth game, an extra-inning nail-chomper won by the heroes of Red Sox Nation, was a 14-inning battle that required 5 hours and 49 minutes to complete. That was 47 minutes longer than Game 4 (12 innings), which was 42 minutes longer than Game 3 (nine innings). All three games set some kind of postseason longevity record.

Add them up and you have 15 hours and 11 minutes of Red Sox-Yankees over three grueling days—with one more to go, at least.

"It's Groundhog Day," Yankees manager Joe Torre said while sitting in the same spot of the same interview room he had occupied only hours earlier while discussing a Game 4 extra-inning loss.

Sometime during Game 5, maybe about the time Mariano Rivera blew his second save in two nights, it became very clear that this series was not over. The Yankees, once three outs away from sweeping the ALCS, were not going to waltz into the World Series. The Red Sox had too much heart to allow that.

And just like in Game 4, Red Sox slugger David Ortiz delivered the biggest blow. This time Boston's "Papi" ended the game with a two-out single off Esteban Loaiza that scored Johnny Damon from second base. Damon, who was struggling through a dreadful series, had reached on a one-out walk and gone to second when Manny

David Ortiz does it again. Boston's lovable 'Papi,' who had hit a home run in the eighth inning, celebrates his 14th-inning single that scores Johnny Damon with the winning run and prompts another wild celebration.

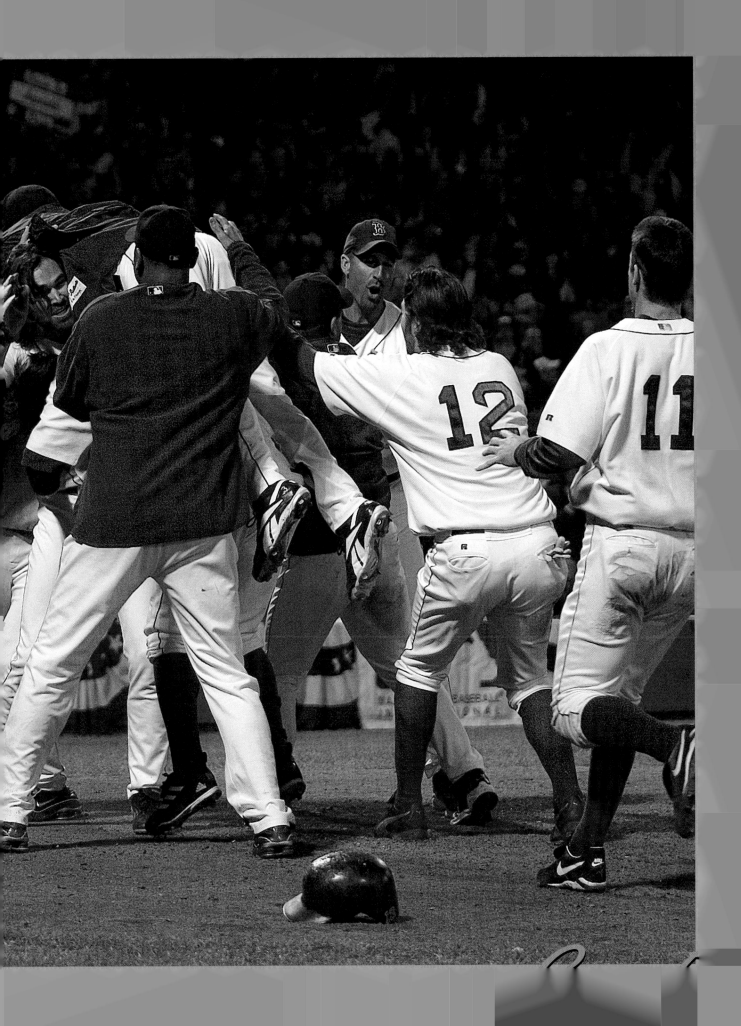

Ramirez walked. Ortiz fouled off six pitches before muscling one to center that broke his bat but brought home Damon.

"The Yankees really have to think about who's their Papi," cracked Red Sox starter Pedro Martinez, referring to Ortiz's nickname—a Spanish term of endearment.

Ortiz, who won Game 4 with a two-run, walkoff homer in the 12th, also started the rally that tied Game 5 in the eighth. The Sox were trailing 4-2 when Ortiz hit a leadoff home run off Tom Gordon. Kevin Millar walked, as he had done to set up the tying rally in Game 4, and a Trot Nixon single brought Rivera in from the bullpen. The first batter he faced, Jason Varitek, lifted a sacrifice fly to center that scored pinch runner Dave Roberts and evened the score heading into the ninth.

While Ortiz was basking in the spotlight, the two Boston wins would not have been possible without gutty performances by the bullpen. Six relievers shut out the Yankees over the final eight innings, one night after five relievers had shut them down over the final six. Knuckleballer Tim Wakefield worked the final three innings for the win, two nights after he had worked 3⅓ innings in a 19-8 loss.

"You can't imagine how happy I am that he gets to end that game," Red Sox manager Terry Francona said. "He pitched the last inning on heart, I mean, I know he had a good knuckleball, but he—everybody was on fumes. You saw two really good teams that really competed with a lot of heart. Thankfully, we're at home and we won."

Wakefield's work was not without adventure. Varitek, who usually gives way to backup catcher Doug Mirabelli when Wakefield pitches, had problems handling the knuckler, a gamble that almost cost Francona. Varitek was charged with three passed balls in the 13th inning, the last of which allowed Hideki Matsui to reach third with one out.

Pedro Martinez pitched six solid innings, but the bullpen was even better. The top four hitters in the Yankees lineup, a combined 2-for-22, struck out eight times, including Alex Rodriguez (bottom).

Singles by Orlando Cabrera (center) and Manny Ramirez (right) set up two first-inning Red Sox runs, the first of which scored on a single by the ever-clutch David Ortiz (left).

Miguel Cairo evades the tag of Jason Varitek to score from first on Derek Jeter's bases-clearing double in the sixth.

But Wakefield retired Bernie Williams on a short fly to right and struck out Ruben Sierra to end the threat. "A gutty son of a gun," Torre said, referring to Wakefield. "I can't say I'm happy he did it, but I certainly respect how he goes about it."

Good outings by both starters practically were forgotten by the end of the night. Yankees righthander Mike Mussina, perfect through six innings in his Game 1 win, was touched for two runs in the first on a single by Ortiz and a bases-loaded walk to Varitek. But he settled down and did not give up another run before departing in the seventh.

Martinez allowed at least one baserunner in each of the first five innings, but still carried a 2-1 lead into the sixth. But true to his recent history, as the pitch count rose, so did the opposition's chances of scoring. Martinez loaded the bases in the sixth by giving up singles to Jorge Posada and Sierra and hitting Miguel Cairo. On his 100th pitch, with two out, Derek Jeter reached out and stroked a bases-clearing double to the opposite field.

Francona kept Martinez in the game and he hit Alex Rodriguez in the left arm and walked Gary Sheffield. But he escaped further damage by getting Matsui on a fly ball to right. The Yankees, up 4-2 after Jeter's hit, were shut out the rest of the way.

"It's still an uphill battle," said Boston first baseman Doug Mientkiewicz. "A lot of people wrote us off already, but we're happy to live and breathe for another day."

Tim Wakefield (above) pitched three innings of scoreless relief and got the win. Five other relievers also shut out the Yankees: (clockwise from top left) Keith Foulke, Mike Timlin, Bronson Arroyo, Alan Embree and Mike Myers.

David Ortiz's home run in the eighth pulled the Red Sox to within one. And later in the inning, pinch-runner Dave Roberts scored the tying run (below left) for the second straight game, this time on Jason Varitek's sacrifice fly. Six grueling innings later, Ortiz struck again—this time with a single that scored Johnny Damon (below right).

Game 6 RED SOX 4, YANKEES 2

All even: Schilling, Bellhorn rescue Sox

Curt Schilling, blood seeping through his sock, gut-checks his way through seven grueling innings while limiting the Yankees to one run and four hits. Mark Bellhorn, a .150 hitter with 10 strikeouts in the A.L. Championship Series, belts a stunning three-run homer off Jon Lieber. The Red Sox, teetering on the edge of elimination for the third straight night, become the first team in baseball history to even up a best-of-seven series after losing the first three games.

If you could write scripts like this, you'd have a mantel covered with best-screenplay Oscars. The incredible Yankees-Red Sox rivalry took another riveting turn in a dramatic, historic Game 6 that once again caused a jump in heart rates all over New England and the Northeast.

The Red Sox, perennial losers in the games that count most between these two teams, used a courageous performance from Schilling to complete their unprecedented turnaround. Boston's hard-fought victory on a cold, damp night at Yankee Stadium defied all odds, set a new standard for comebacks and sent the ALCS snowballing into a monumental seventh game.

A week after a hobbling Schilling was punished by the Yankees in their 10-7 series-opening win, the big righthander hoisted the Sox on his back. With his splitter showing good bite and his fastball reaching 94 mph—about 4 mph faster than his Game 1 start—Schilling retired the first eight Yankees hitters and allowed only one runner to reach third before giving up a bases-empty home run to Bernie Williams in the seventh. Schilling departed in pain, with the Red Sox

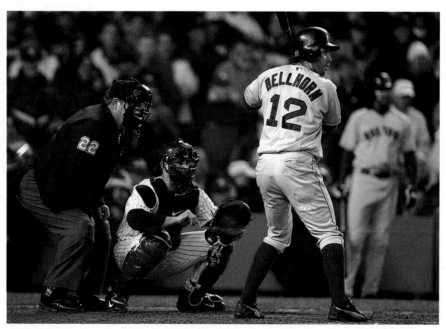

Curt Schilling, carrying the Red Sox's pennant dreams on his back, ignored the pain of his injured ankle and pitched seven strong innings. Mark Bellhorn broke out of his horrid slump with a critical three-run homer.

leading, 4-1.

He was pitching, it later was revealed, with a tendon that had dislocated from a bone in his right ankle. He said the Red Sox's medical staff had performed a procedure during which they sewed skin in his leg to tissue underneath, creating a wall that would keep the affected tendon from popping in and out of place. If the tendon had not been stabilized, Schilling risked it being frayed or even torn. The blood was visible early in the game; his movements were tentative whenever he had to make a defensive play. Schilling, admitting he never felt like his usual self, said he struggled from the fourth inning on.

But a struggling Schilling was good enough. And though temptation to keep him in the game must have been overwhelming, Red Sox manager Terry Francona did not hesitate to remove him before the eighth inning, even though Schilling had thrown only 94 pitches.

"When you see Schill tell the umpire after the inning 'good job,'" said Francona, referring to Schilling's gesture as he walked off the mound after pitching the seventh, "I'm not sending him back out. He's had it. That was plenty."

Schilling wasn't the only hero on this night. The struggling Bellhorn, who had been dropped from second in the order to ninth, hit his opposite-field homer off Lieber to complete the scoring in a four-run fourth inning. The home run hit a fan in the first row of the left field seats and bounced back into play. Left fielder Hideki Matsui picked up the ball and threw to second where Bellhorn stood, not sure whether to stay or circle the bases. The umpires consulted and awarded Bellhorn his home run.

The umpires had to gather again in the eighth to decide a disputed play. After Derek Jeter singled in a run to trim the Sox lead to 4-2, Alex Rodriguez dribbled

With blood oozing from his sock (inset) even before the start of Game 6, Curt Schilling flashed a mid-90s fastball and a determination that carried the Red Sox to a critical stay-alive victory.

Kevin Millar's fourth-inning double (above) and Jason Varitek's single produced one run, but the big blow was Mark Bellhorn's three-run, opposite-field homer that bounced off a fan and back onto the field, where it was picked up by left fielder Hideki Matsui (55).

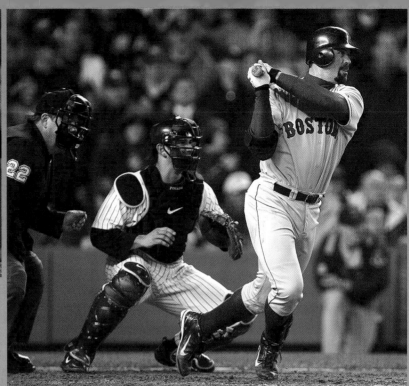

a grounder toward first base. Sox pitcher Bronson Arroyo fielded the ball and reached his glove hand to tag a sprinting A-Rod, who took a chopping swing at Arroyo's glove and dislodged the ball, which rolled down the right field line. Jeter circled the bases and A-Rod ended up on second as Francona hustled out of the dugout to contest the no-call.

Again the umpires huddled and again they made a controversial (by Yankee Stadium crowd standards) reversal, ruling correctly that Rodriguez was out because of interference and Jeter had to return to first. Instead of being down 4-3 with a runner on second and one out, the Yankees still trailed 4-2 with two out and Jeter on first.

"I had a problem with (the call) because (first base umpire) Randy Marsh was closer than anybody else and it was like it was bodies all over the place," Yankees manager Joe Torre said. "First off, they said that Arroyo was in motion, too; it's not like he was standing there. And there was also a player on the Red Sox who was in the line that didn't have the ball, which can be an obstruction play. So there are a lot of things that went on that didn't fall our way. That's the way it goes."

Red Sox closer Keith Foulke continued his sensational postseason work by pitching a scoreless ninth to save the victory. When the game ended, catcher Jason Varitek jumped into Foulke's arms as the Red Sox congratulated one another for the third straight night.

"I am so freaking proud to be a part of this team," Schilling said. "These guys are phenomenal. I'm just so proud to be a part of this team. We just did something that has never been done. It ain't over by any stretch against this team and this organization. … I'm feeling pretty special about being a part of this club right now."

No wonder. Being the star of a story too amazing to make up can have that effect.

Boston pitcher Bronson Arroyo reaches to tag Alex Rodriguez, who raises his arm in an attempt to knock the ball free. A-Rod succeeded, a play that was ruled interference and helped the Red Sox post a critical win in Game 6.

Curt Schilling (left) was miserable because of his painful ankle injury. Derek Jeter was miserable for entirely different reasons.

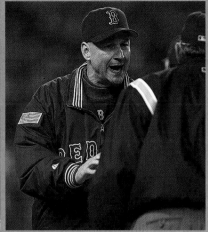

Orlando Cabrera (far left) and manager Terry Francona (left) voice complaints about the A-Rod interference controversy, which prompted the umpires to huddle and reverse their ruling, much to the dismay of Yankees manager Joe Torre, Rodriguez and New York fans, who drew the attention of riot police.

The Yankees couldn't respond to their fans' call for a rally in the ninth as Keith Foulke closed them down, prompting a hug from Jason Varitek and grateful handshakes between Francona and his players.

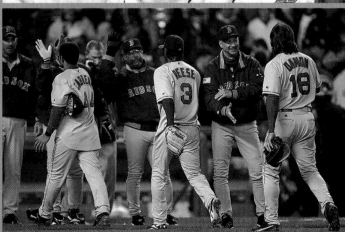

Game 7   RED SOX 10, YANKEES 3

They're back! Red Sox return to World Series

On the very same field where their hearts had been broken a year earlier, the Red Sox celebrated. They celebrated the rush of becoming the first major league team to come back from a 3-0 deficit to win a best-of-seven postseason series. They celebrated their chance to represent Boston in a World Series for the first time in 18 years. And they celebrated a victory over the hated Yankees—a rather lopsided 10-3 win that touched the soul of Red Sox Nation.

"Last year, we had a bad memory," said David Ortiz, the most valuable player in the A.L. Championship Series. "A lot of my teammates were just destroyed because we played a pretty good (ALCS Game 7 in 2003) and we lost and it was a big-time opportunity to step to the World Series. … We saw a lot of fans crying and feeling hurt and I

think myself and all of my teammates, we were worried about it. And that's one of the big reasons for us to come to the field and represent (Boston) the way we did the last four games."

This time, unlike so many other times in this great rivalry, no dramatic finish was needed. Ortiz blasted a two-run homer in the first and Johnny Damon hit a grand slam in the second to put the Red Sox in control, 6-0. From that point on, fans throughout New England counted down every out.

Red Sox sinkerballer Derek Lowe, a free agent-to-be who was not expected to return to Boston, allowed only one hit in six innings—a Derek Jeter single that scored the Yankees' first run in the third. Working on two days rest, Lowe walked only one before turning the final three innings over to the bullpen. Lowe, who was not in the postseason rotation

<table>
<tr><td></td><td colspan="9"></td><td>R</td><td>H</td><td>E</td><td></td></tr>
<tr><td>BOSTON</td><td>240</td><td>200</td><td>011</td><td>10</td><td>13</td><td>0</td><td>W: LOWE (1-0, 3.18)</td></tr>
<tr><td>NEW YORK</td><td>001</td><td>000</td><td>200</td><td>3</td><td>5</td><td>1</td><td>L: BROWN (0-1, 21.60)</td></tr>
</table>

Johnny Damon (above right) did serious damage with two home runs and an LCS record-tying six RBIs, prompting catcher Jason Varitek and reliever Alan Embree to do serious celebrating after the Red Sox's Game 7 win.

because of a dismal September, made his way back into the club's good graces with 5⅓ solid innings in Game 4—the victory that started the historic comeback. Lowe started that game only because the Sox used up six pitchers in a 19-8 Game 3 loss at Femway Park.

"When someone tells you that you really can't do something that you think you can, given an opportunity, you want to go out there and prove to yourself that you can do it," Lowe said. "There was a lot in this series for me personally. You go out there and you just try to pitch well. … Games like this can make or break your so-called career and I know a lot of people in Boston have been talking about this whole free-agency thing and keep saying, is this going to be your last game? You know, luckily, it's not going to be."

Damon, who capped a huge night with a two-run homer in the fourth, also had a lot on the line individually. The leadoff man had struggled mightily in the first six games, going 3-for-29 with four strikeouts in the opener. "Good players step up," Damon said, "and I'm a good player."

Yankees starter Kevin Brown retired only four batters and was charged with five runs as Yankee pitchers, who had struggled since the All-Star break, let the team down at the most inopportune time. The Sox roughed up six pitchers for 13 hits and worked them for seven walks.

"You go out there and all of a sudden you give up a two-spot and a four-spot and that's a hell of a hill to climb," Yankees manager Joe Torre said. "Fact is, even if you try to fight your way back, Derek Lowe did another great job for them. If we scored a run, they scored two; we scored two, they scored one. So we could never really mount anything to get back into it. We just didn't pitch well enough."

The Yankees mounted only one serious rally. In the seventh, with the Sox already leading 8-1, Pedro Martinez

Fireworks started quickly for the Red Sox when Johnny Damon singled to lead off the game, stole second (above) and was thrown out at the plate (center) trying to score on a Manny Ramirez single. When David Ortiz followed with a home run, the Sox had a 2-0 lead.

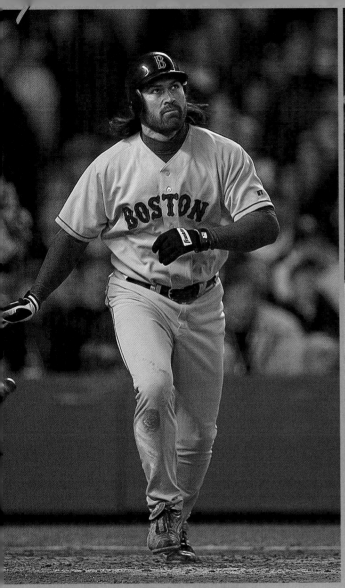

After starter Kevin Brown loaded the bases in the second inning, Joe Torre pulled him (left) for Javier Vazquez, who served up a grand slam to Johnny Damon (above, top right). That was plenty of support for Derek Lowe, who allowed only one hit in six innings.

relieved Lowe and gave up back-to-back doubles to Hideki Matsui and Bernie Williams and a single to Kenny Lofton. But with two on and only one out, Martinez struck out John Olerud and retired Miguel Cairo on a fly to right.

Mark Bellhorn, who also had been fighting a postseason slump, quickly turned the Yankees' seventh-inning momentum by hitting a leadoff homer in the eighth off Tom Gordon.

The Red Sox did not even need to call on closer Keith Foulke. Mike Timlin worked a scoreless 1⅔ innings and Alan Embree got the final out.

"We won this as a ballclub. We'll celebrate as a ballclub and we'll move on as a ballclub," said Red Sox manager Terry Francona.

With an ecstatic Red Sox Nation cheering their every move.

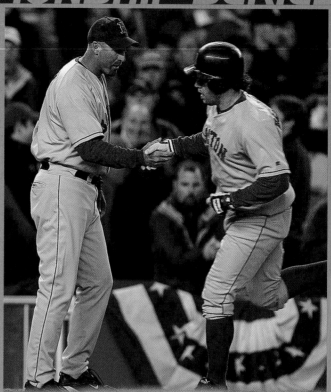

After Johnny Damon's second home run of the game (below) and Mark Bellhorn's solo shot (right) in the eighth inning, Red Sox fans were understandably giddy. The Boston dugout also was giddy in the ninth when reliever Mike Timlin was pulled (below right) with two out and the Sox leading, 10-3.

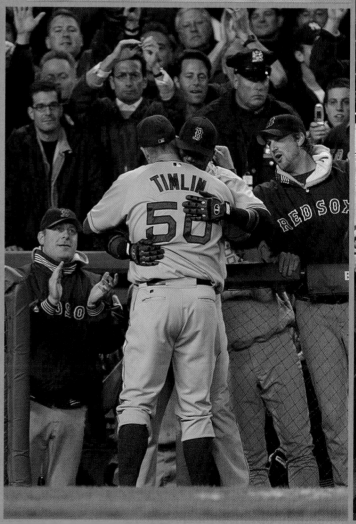

When the final out was recorded pitcher Derek Lowe (above) join teammates and fans in celebrat Red Sox's historic victory.

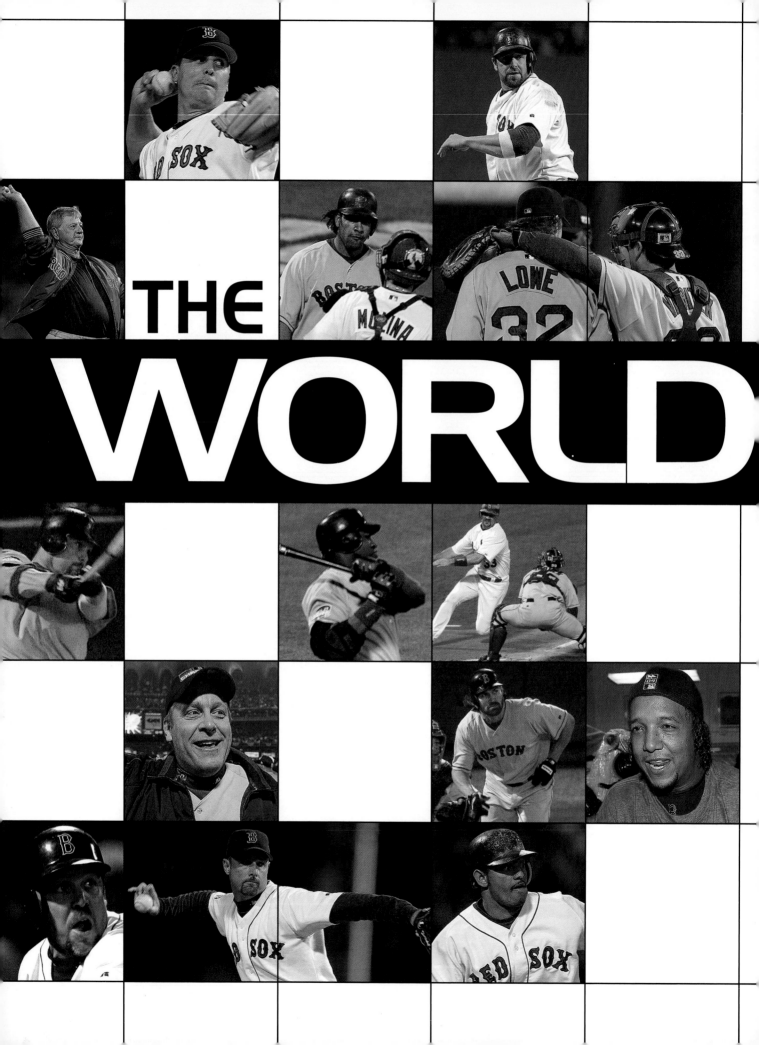

THE WORLD

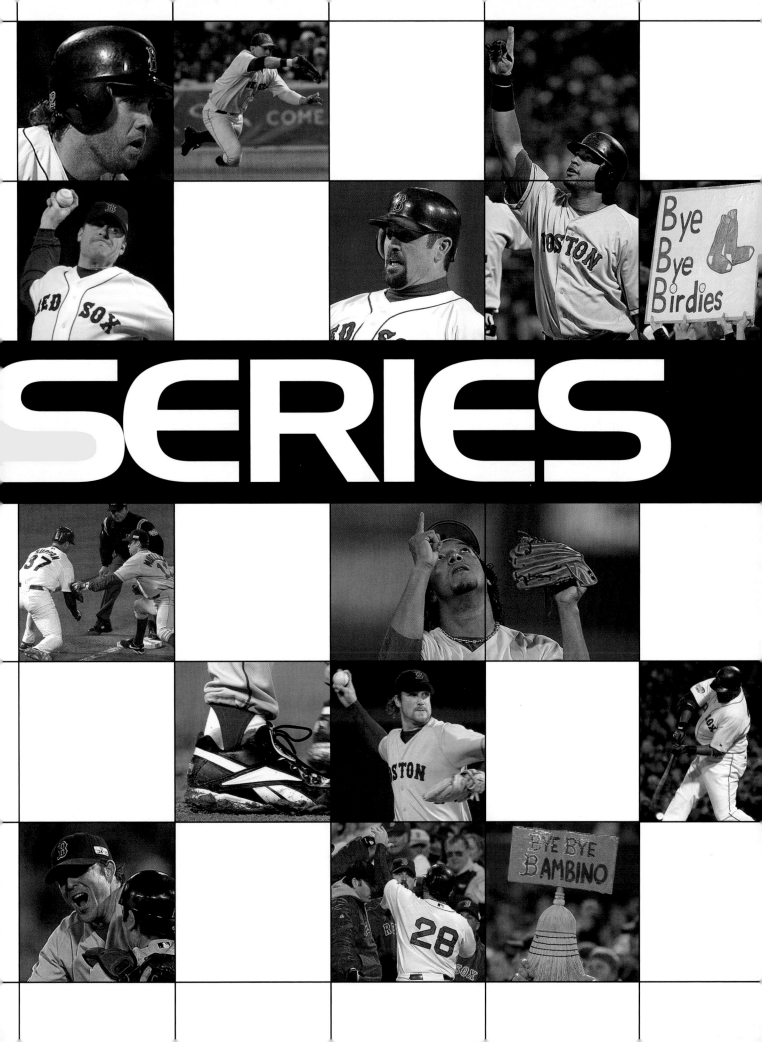

SERIES

Game 1 — RED SOX 11, CARDINALS 9

Bellhorn's home run decides Series opener

After the Red Sox and Cardinals survived seven-game League Championship Series that were as draining as they were thrilling, one of the biggest questions entering the World Series was this: Which team would reset its intensity meter the fastest?

It didn't take long to get that answer. In the first inning of their first World Series game since 1986, the Red Sox pounced. Two of their first three hitters reached base off St. Louis starter Woody Williams, and David Ortiz added to his growing Boston legend by blasting a pitch to right field, a drive that hooked just inside the foul pole for a three-run homer. After Bill Mueller added an RBI single to make it 4-0, it was clear the Red Sox still had plenty of momentum from their record-setting

ALCS victory over the Yankees.

After three innings, Boston's lead had swelled to 7-2, with Johnny Damon, Orlando Cabrera and Manny Ramirez supplying RBIs. But this laugher took a bizarre turn, thanks to shoddy execution, walks and poor defense on both sides. In fact, the game had an unkempt look that bore a fitting resemblance to many of the scraggly Sox players.

Boston starter Tim Wakefield lost control of his fluttering knuckler in the fourth, when he walked four. Add in a passed ball and a throwing error by first baseman Kevin Millar, and you get three runs on one hit—and a much-tighter 7-5 game.

Then in the sixth, the Cardinals staged a two-out rally and tied the score at 7, thanks to RBI doubles by Edgar

ST. LOUIS	011	302	020		9	11	1	
BOSTON	403	000	22X		11	13	4	

W: FOULKE (1-0, 0.00)
L: TAVAREZ (0-1, 9.00)

The Red Sox played long ball with the Cardinals, scoring three first-inning runs on a stunning blow by David Ortiz, and a pair of eighth-inning runs on a back-breaker by Mark Bellhorn (12), who is shown getting a high five from Jason Varitek.

Renteria and Larry Walker, a 16-year veteran whose first World Series game included four hits and a home run.

"We were maybe overexcited," Red Sox manager Terry Francona said. "I don't think the players were nervous, but they were making me nervous."

Mistakes were not limited to the Red Sox. Cardinals reliever Kiko Calero walked Mark Bellhorn and Orlando Cabrera in the seventh—two of the eight free passes issued by St. Louis pitchers. Ramirez gave the Sox an 8-7 lead with a sharp single to center that scored Bellhorn. The Cardinals called on lefthanded specialist Ray King to face Ortiz, who grounded hard to second baseman Tony Womack. The ball took a late, wicked hop and struck Womack in the collarbone, forcing him from the game and allowing Cabrera to score on the infield single.

Defense—again—betrayed Boston in the eighth. With two on, Renteria singled to left. Ramirez fumbled the ball, allowing pinch runner Jason Marquis, who had stopped at third, to score. The next hitter, Walker, lofted a fly to left. Ramirez, attempting a sliding catch, caught his spikes in the grass and the ball bounced off his glove as he tumbled to the ground, allowing Roger Cedeno to score. Albert Pujols was walked intentionally, loading the bases. But Keith Foulke retired Scott Rolen on a popout and Jim Edmonds on a strikeout.

Entering Boston's half of the eighth, the score was 9-9. With one out, Jason Varitek reached on yet another error—this one by shortstop Renteria. That brought up Bellhorn, who turned on a Julian Tavarez pitch that caught too

After Sox legend Carl Yastrzemski (inset) threw out the ceremonial first pitch, Tim Wakefield turned his knuckleball loose on the Cardinals. He wasn't sharp, but he did hold their 3-4-5 hitters to one hit—a bunt single by Jim Edmonds.

Johnny Damon got things started for the Red Sox in the first inning with a leadoff double (left), and Orlando Cabrera (44) was hit by a pitch. David Ortiz's three-run homer provided an early indication this would be a short night for Cardinals starter Woody Williams.

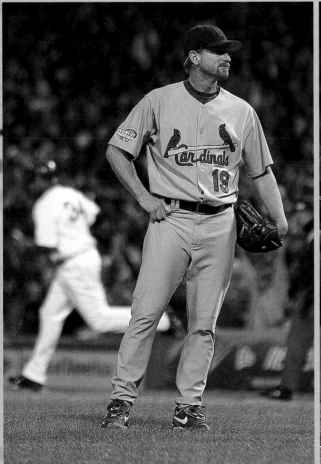

Bellhorn: 2-for-3, HR, 3 R, 2 RBIs

Kevin Millar doubled (above left) and scored on Bill Mueller's first-inning single. Two innings later, Johnny Damon's bases-loaded single (below) drove in a run and prompted a Cardinals' pitching change. Larry Walker was a one-man wrecking crew for the Cardinals, going 4-for-5 with a home run.

much of the plate. With Fenway Park fans holding their collective breath, the ball hit the right field foul pole, prompting Red Sox players to spill out of the dugout in a wild celebration as Bellhorn circled the bases.

This was the same Bellhorn who hit .091 in the A.L. Division Series against Anaheim and struggled for much of the LCS before hitting a key Game 6 homer.

"I think we forget that the mind is a powerful thing and sometimes we just lose our confidence," Bellhorn said of his earlier playoff struggles. "You want to win so bad that you put too much pressure on yourself. You just got to battle through it and that's what I did."

The Red Sox held the lead this time, although the Cardinals did put the tying run on base in the ninth following a one-out double by Marlon Anderson. But this strange game of give-and-take finally ended when Foulke retired the final two hitters, including Cedeno on a victory-sealing strikeout. It wasn't artistic, but in the end, it didn't need to be.

"That was not an instructional video," Francona said of the often sloppy play. "That was a little rough. We did some things wrong, but we persevered and we won."

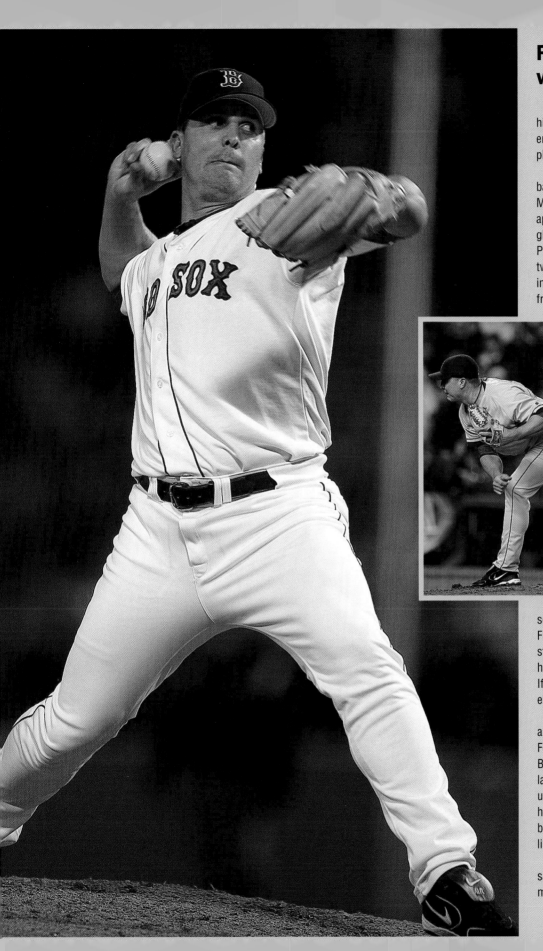

Foulke steadies Sox when Cardinals rally

In a game that featured 20 runs, 24 hits, 14 walks, two hit batsmen and five errors, Red Sox closer Keith Foulke supplied a little normalcy.

After the Cardinals tied the score on back-to-back errors by Sox left fielder Manny Ramirez, Foulke did not come apart; instead, he proved to be Boston's glue. After intentionally walking Albert Pujols to load the bases, Foulke got the two most important outs of the game, inducing Scott Rolen to pop to third and freezing Jim Edmonds with a called third strike on the inside corner. Then, after Boston grabbed an 11-9 lead in the bottom of the inning, Foulke closed the door on the Cardinals in the ninth, striking out two, including Roger Cedeno to end the game.

"I mean, Foulke made some pitches," Sox manager Terry Francona said. "It's easy when things start going wrong, to kind of put your head down or even feel sorry for yourself. If the Cardinals take the lead (in the eighth), that's a whole different game."

Though he may lack the star power of an Eric Gagne or a Mariano Rivera, Foulke's presence in the back end of Boston's bullpen gives it a dimension it lacked last season. His stunning change-up makes him equally difficult on left-handers and righthanders, and his durability allows him to pitch multiple innings, like in Game 1.

"He's a huge, huge weapon for us," said Francona. "Foulke can do so much. I mean, he'll take the ball all the time."

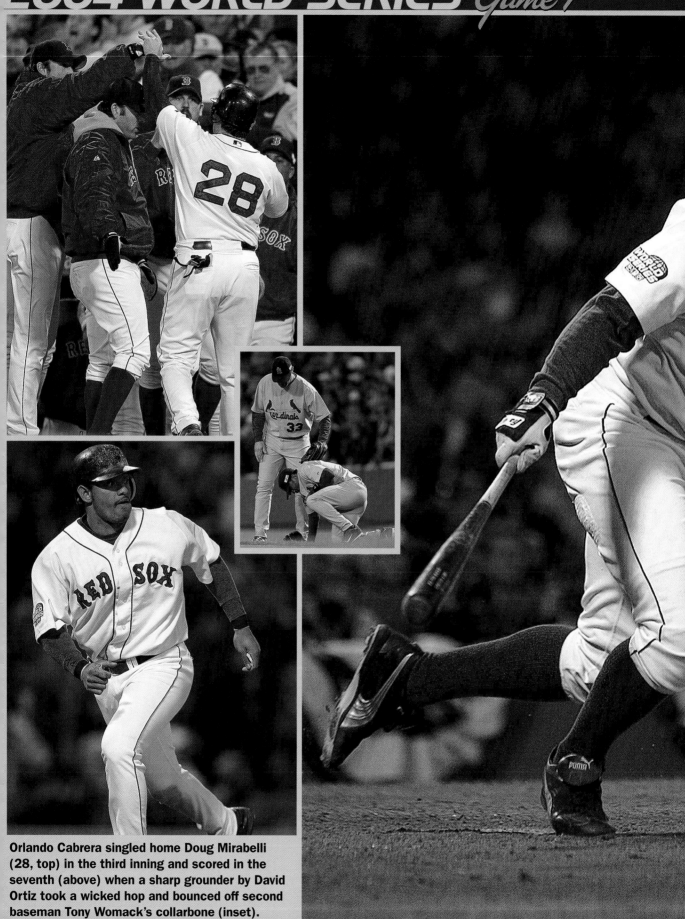

Orlando Cabrera singled home Doug Mirabelli (28, top) in the third inning and scored in the seventh (above) when a sharp grounder by David Ortiz took a wicked hop and bounced off second baseman Tony Womack's collarbone (inset).

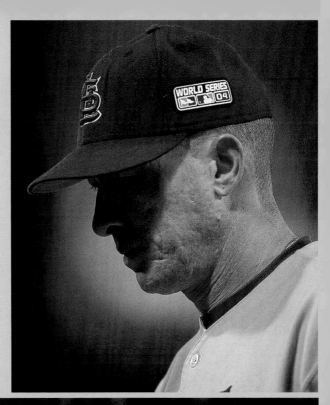

Mark Bellhorn (left) watches the flight of his game-deciding two-run homer in the bottom of the eighth inning—a shot that hit Pesky's Pole down the right field line and made a loser out of Julian Tavarez (right). The runs were all Keith Foulke needed to close out the victory and earn a victory hug.

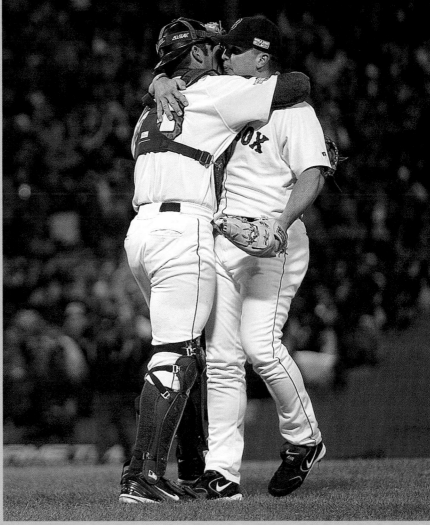

Game 2 — RED SOX 6, CARDINALS 2

Injured Schilling ties Cardinals in stitches

Curt Schilling, who made $12 million in 2004, didn't come cheap. Neither did his talk. Instead of shrinking from pressure, Schilling invited it by saying the only reason he was wearing a Red Sox uniform was to bring a world championship to Boston.

With the drama of a made-for-TV movie—Schilling had stitches placed in his right ankle between playoff starts and pitched on as blood soaked through his sock during games—he continued to keep Boston on course. Schilling might not have been as sharp in Game 2 of the World Series as he was in beating the Yankees in Game 6 of the ALCS, but he allowed the Cardinals only one unearned run and four hits in six gutty innings, and the Red Sox claimed a 2-0 series lead.

Schilling, who pitched against the Yankees just days after it was announced he probably would not pitch again in the postseason because of a damaged tendon in his right ankle, said he was in such pain when he woke up on the morning of World Series Game 2 that he "couldn't walk, couldn't move." But he was inspired by his drive to the game.

"There were signs every mile from my house to this ballpark, on fire stations, on telephone poles, wishing me luck," he said.

Then, Boston's medical staff went to work at Fenway. A stitch was removed that had caught a nerve in his ankle, and

<table>
<tr><td rowspan="2">ST. LOUIS</td><td>000</td><td>100</td><td>010</td><td>2</td><td>5</td><td>0</td></tr>
</table>

ST. LOUIS   000 100 010   2 5 0

BOSTON   200 202 00X   6 8 4

L: MORRIS (0-1, 8.31)
W: SCHILLING (1-0, 0.00)

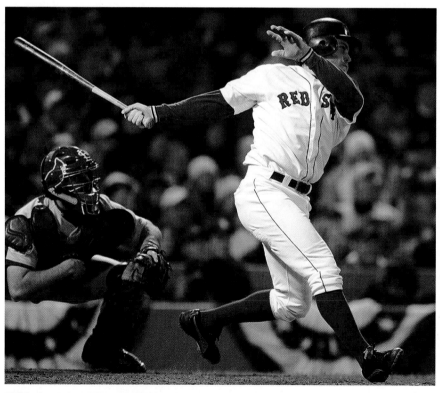

With Curt Schilling battling through six four-hit innings and Game 1 hero Mark Bellhorn delivering a two-run double, the Red Sox grabbed a 2-0 World Series lead by sweeping at Fenway Park.

2004 WORLD SERIES

Game 2

his condition improved dramatically.

Though he labored, Schilling shut down a potent—yet slumping—Cardinals offense.

"You could see Curt was battling," Boston manager Terry Francona said. "But he was very, very good."

Schilling weaved in and out of trouble. He pitched around a double by Albert Pujols in the first inning, and he got Mike Matheny to line into a double play with two on and one out in the second. He was aided in that inning when Reggie Sanders missed the bag while rounding second base and had to retreat instead of advancing to third on a ball hit into the gap by Tony Womack.

In the fifth, Schilling got another double play. And in the sixth, he pitched around two more errors by a leaky Red Sox defense.

Though his velocity wasn't up to usual standards, Schilling, who also sustained an injury to his hip in the third inning, relied on location and a sharp split-finger pitch.

"I thought early on, he wasn't quite as sharp," St. Louis manager Tony La Russa said. "After that, whenever we even got a smell, he made quality pitches."

For the second straight night, Red Sox hitters jumped on the Cardinals' starter. After Matt Morris retired the first two hitters, he walked Boston's big guns, Manny Ramirez and David Ortiz. Those were the ninth and 10th walks issued to Boston in its first 10 innings. Jason Varitek made Morris pay with a two-run triple.

St. Louis got a run in the fourth when Pujols doubled for the second time, moved to third on a flyout and scored on one of third baseman Bill Mueller's three errors.

In the first two games, the Cardinals had trouble building momentum and putting together rallies without the help of Boston's defense. Pujols collected three hits in Game 2, but he didn't drive in a run in the first two games. Rolen didn't have a hit; Jim Edmonds, the Cardinals' third N.L. MVP candidate, had only a bunt single. Collectively, their only RBI was produced by Rolen's eighth-inning sacrifice fly in

Orlando Cabrera's sixth inning shot off the Green Monster drove in two runs and gave Red Sox fans increasing reason to believe that the curse, indeed, was being reversed.

Bill Mueller had a tough night defensively, but he also led the Red Sox with two hits.

Game 2.

While the Cardinals' big bats were quiet, the Red Sox continued to get clutch hits up and down their order. After St. Louis pulled to within 2-1 in the top of the fourth, Boston answered with two runs in the bottom of the inning when Kevin Millar, who was hit by a pitch, and Mueller, who had doubled, scored on a double by Mark Bellhorn, the hero of Game 1. A two-run single off the Green Monster by Orlando Cabrera in the sixth added further insurance for the Red Sox.

The win marked the ninth time in Boston's first 12 postseason games that it had scored six or more runs.

"There's no letdown in this lineup," said Red Sox setup man Alan Embree, who teamed with fellow setup man Mike Timlin and closer Keith Foulke to close out the Cardinals over the final three innings.

That gave the win to Schilling, who clearly was the story of this game. "I just wish everybody on this planet could experience the day that I just experienced," he said.

The Sox had their defensive ups and downs. Right fielder Trot Nixon made a nice catch (above) and third baseman Bill Mueller doubled up Reggie Sanders (below) after catching a line drive. But Mueller also made three errors, one on a foul pop collision with catcher Jason Varitek.

Catcher Jason Varitek was a guiding force through Game 2. He delivered the defining hit, a first-inning triple that drove in two runs, then helped Curt Schilling execute during his masterful and gutty performance.

Masked man Varitek steps up big

Manny Ramirez and David Ortiz, unquestionably, were the stars of the Red Sox's offense. But it was catcher Jason Varitek who supplied the defining hit in Game 2.

And while the headlines and cameras all focused on the gallant performance of Curt Schilling, it was Varitek who guided him along behind the plate.

Varitek didn't start Game 1 of the World Series because his back-up, Doug Mirabelli, is better at catching the tricky knuckleball of Tim Wakefield. But Varitek made his presence felt immediately in Game 2. After Cardinals starter Matt Morris walked Ramirez and Ortiz in the first, Varitek hammered a 1-2 pitch off the wall in the quirky triangle area in Fenway Park's center field, just to the right of the 420-foot sign. That gave Boston a 2-0 lead, kept the Cardinals backpedaling and allowed the banged-up Schilling a little cushion.

The message was clear: You can pitch around Ramirez and Ortiz—at your own risk.

"With Varitek," manager Terry Francona said, "that gives us an added dimension, another weapon in the middle of that order."

Schilling, who lacked his dominant stuff, relied on the heady Varitek to show him the way and pace him as he pitched through pain.

"Jason is a guy that I feed off," Schilling said. "I know he's putting down the fingers he believes in. I know he's got an idea, every time, every pitch, every at-bat."

Varitek, who hit .296 with 18 homers and 73 RBIs in the regular season, is productive offensively and respected defensively. That's a rarity for his position. Varitek isn't the most valuable Sox player, but he's close. And, without question, he's the team's heart and soul. Game 2 demonstrated that.

Curt Schilling, who didn't think there was any way he could pitch when he woke up on the morning of Game 2, beat the Cardinals on sheer will and determination, qualities he has demonstrated often over the years.

Having vanquished the 'Birdies' in Fenway Park, Johnny Damon (18), Manny Ramirez (below left), Keith Foulke, Jason Varitek and their Red Sox teammates headed their history-making roadshow to St. Louis.

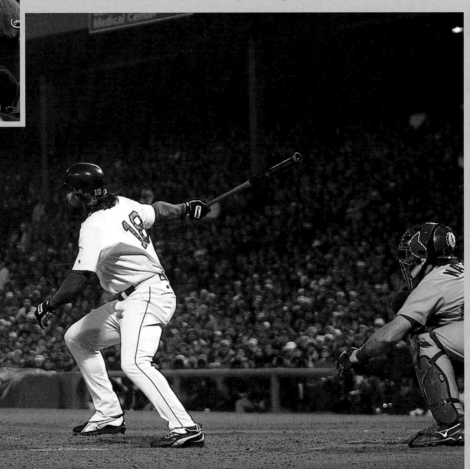

Game 3 — RED SOX 4, CARDINALS 1

Pedro, Manny efforts put Red Sox on brink

During their respective stints in Boston, Pedro Martinez and Manny Ramirez had been alternately dazzling and confounding. At Martinez's best, he had been the most dominant pitcher in baseball. At his worst, he had called the hated Yankees his "daddy." Ramirez was known for hitting a baseball as hard, as consistently and as productively as anyone. But at his worst, he went unclaimed on waivers because of his too-high salary and sometimes flighty play.

But in helping the Red Sox grab a stranglehold of their first World Series title in 86 years, Pedro and Manny, as they are known in Boston, showed why they were worth the trouble.

The more Martinez pitched in Game 3, the less of a clue the Cardinals had of how to hit him.

And with each of Ramirez's World Series at-bats, the less of a clue they had of how to get him out.

After falling into an 0-2 series hole in Boston, the Cardinals pinned their hopes on a return to St. Louis, where they were 6-0 in the postseason. But Ramirez tempered that zest early. After Johnny Damon and Orlando Cabrera were retired on hard-hit balls to the outfield, Ramirez came to the plate. With the count 2-2 and the Busch Stadium crowd standing and roaring for a strikeout, St. Louis starter Jeff Suppan left a pitch up and Ramirez pounded it into the left field loge section for a 1-0 Red Sox lead.

"I'm just trying to relax at the plate, just trying to get a good pitch to hit, and I got it and I just went deep," Ramirez said.

It appeared that Martinez, who was making the first World Series start of his illustrious career, might not protect that early cushion. After retiring leadoff hitter Edgar Renteria, Martinez walked

After Pedro Martinez escaped tough jams in the first and third innings, he settled into a groove and retired the last 14 Cardinals he faced. He got plenty of support from Manny Ramirez, who homered in the first and singled home a later run.

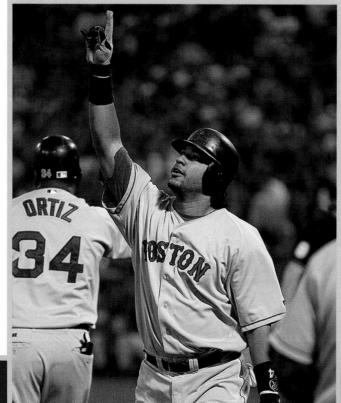

				W: MARTINEZ (1-0, 0.00)
				L: SUPPAN (0-1, 7.71)
BOSTON	100 120 000	4 9 0	
ST. LOUIS	000 000 001	1 4 0	

Larry Walker, allowed a single to Albert Pujols and walked Scott Rolen on five pitches. Twice, catcher Jason Varitek went to the mound to offer counsel. And Martinez finally silenced the crowd by getting Jim Edmonds on a short flyout to Ramirez, who threw out Walker trying to score from third to end the inning.

Martinez needed another double play—set up by a baserunning gaffe by Suppan—to avert trouble in the third after allowing a hit to the Cardinals pitcher and a double to Renteria. With one out, Walker hit a roller to second baseman Mark Bellhorn, who was conceding the run. But Suppan started home, stopped, took a step back toward third, stopped again, took a step toward home and then reversed a final time and headed for third. David Ortiz, who had recorded the out at first, fired to Bill Mueller, who tagged Suppan out.

Given a second reprieve, Martinez settled into a groove. And the Red Sox again showed off their deep and relentless lineup. After Ortiz and Varitek were retired in the fourth, Mueller doubled to left-center field, and on the next pitch, Trot Nixon singled him home to make it 2-0.

Suppan wouldn't make it out of the fifth. He allowed a leadoff double to Damon and a single to Cabrera. That brought up Ramirez, and he burned the Cardinals again. After falling behind 0-2, Ramirez took a ball before singling to left for his sixth hit in 12 at-bats and second RBI of the game. Mueller capped the fifth with another big hit— this one chased Suppan—to make it 4-0. With Martinez in top form, it might as well have been 14-0. The Cardinals, who seemed to be wheezing after running themselves out of scoring opportunities in the first and third innings, only could flail at Martinez's offerings. From the third inning until he departed after seven, Martinez retired 14 straight hitters. He closed like a champion. Starting with the

Jeff Suppan gave up a first-inning home run to Manny Ramirez (right) and an RBI single to Trot Nixon (far right) in the fourth. Suppan was pulled in the fifth.

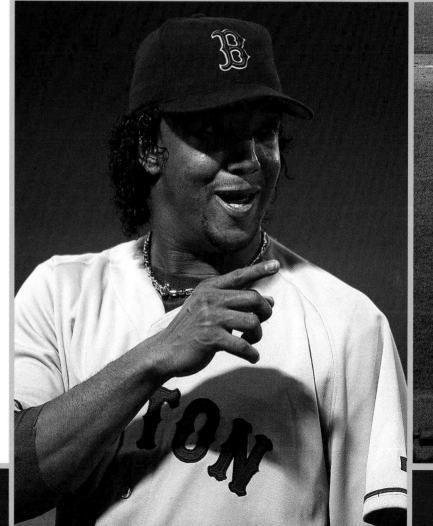

Pedro Martinez (far left) had reason to smile during a seven-inning effort in which he held Jim Edmonds (left) and the rest of the Cardinals to three hits.

Cardinals' top of the lineup in the sixth, Martinez mowed through the final six hitters without the ball leaving the infield, with Pujols, Edmonds and Reggie Sanders striking out.

"I thought he mixed things well, location, speeds, what the ball was doing," St. Louis manager Tony La Russa said, referring to Martinez. "He gave our club a lot of different looks, and I didn't see him throw too many balls over the middle."

Mike Timlin took over in the eighth and recorded three ground-ball outs, and closer Keith Foulke pitched the ninth. Foulke allowed a solo homer to Walker with one out, but got Pujols to fly out and Rolen on a strikeout.

With the Red Sox one win away from a World Series championship, Ramirez and Martinez flapped their hair, which they agreed to let grow long, and pointed toward the sky.

"That's the way we congratulate each other and we thank God for whatever good deed we had done on the field," Martinez said. "We do it our own way. That's just Manny being Manny and Pedro being Pedro."

And their way was too much for the Cardinals.

Orlando Cabrera, like the Red Sox fans, had reason to believe somebody up there was looking out for them. Cabrera got two hits and scored a run in the Game 3 victory.

When Larry Walker tried to score from third on a short fly ball to left fielder Manny Ramirez in the first, he was cut down at the plate (left). In the third, Jeff Suppan was tagged out at third after his indecision on a ground ball hit to second.

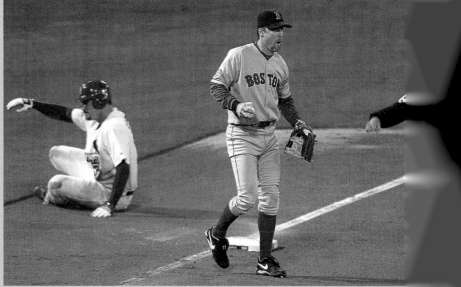

Shaky defense rises to the occasion at Busch Stadium

With the bases loaded and one out in the first inning, the Cardinals' Jim Edmonds lofted a fly ball to shallow left field. Manny Ramirez, who had committed two slapstick errors in Game 1, caught it and made a strong, albeit short, throw home to nail Larry Walker, who had aggressively tagged and tried to score from third.

Two innings later, Cardinals pitcher Jeff Suppan reached on a swinging bunt and advanced to third on a double by Edgar Renteria. That ball eluded right fielder Trot Nixon, who slid on the water-logged warning track of rain-soaked Busch Stadium.

With Boston's infield back, Walker hit a roller to second baseman Mark Bellhorn, who threw to David Ortiz for the out. That should have easily scored Suppan, but he stopped after making a break for home, thinking third base coach Jose Oquendo yelled "No," instead of "Go." Ortiz alertly noticed Suppan's hesitation and threw to Bill Mueller, who tagged out Suppan for a double play.

When the series shifted from Fenway, it was believed the shaky fielding of the Red Sox, who committed eight errors in the first two games, would be further exposed because Busch Stadium is a bigger park and the lumbering Ortiz would have to play in the field because the DH isn't used in N.L. stadiums.

And while neither Martinez's nor Ortiz's play would have drawn votes for Gold Glove consideration, each was executed without incident and ended the Cardinals' only two significant uprisings. Simply, they were the two biggest plays of the game.

Ramirez and Ortiz are special because of their bats. But, in this game, it didn't hurt the Sox to have their arms around, either.

The World Series was not kind to Albert Pujols (right) and the Cardinals. But the Sox enjoyed their experience, whether watching from a prime dugout seat like Kevin Millar or simply hanging with a friend like Manny Ramirez and Orlando Cabrera. For Bill Mueller (below right) a nice play was the ticket.

Red Sox starter Pedro Martinez was in total control after the third inning while Cardinals starter Jeff Suppan was gone before the fifth inning ended.

Game 3 ended as so many other Sox postseason games had—with Keith Foulke on the mound and another dejected player, this time Scott Rolen, walking away.

Game 4 RED SOX 3, CARDINALS 0

No curse: Red Sox simply were the best

For the Red Sox to end their world championship drought, they didn't need an elaborate exorcism or the presence of some supernatural force. Instead, a ground ball back to the pitcher, followed by an underhanded toss to first, did the trick. An apocalypse didn't accompany the final out. Instead, all that happened was a group of big-hearted, high-character players with special talent swarmed the field at St. Louis' Busch Stadium to celebrate a World Series title.

The 2004 Boston Red Sox didn't win their first title since 1918 because they finally overcame some curse; they won it because they were the best team in baseball. That this World Series ended with Edgar Renteria meekly tapping out to Keith Foulke was fitting, for this four-game sweep was an exercise in total domination. Consider:

■ The Red Sox scored in the first inning of each game. They hit more home runs in that inning (three) than the Cardinals hit in the entire series (two).

■ The Cardinals, who won a big-league-best 105 games in the regular season, didn't hold a lead in the entire series. Not once.

■ Red Sox pitchers completely shut down the National League's best offense during the regular season. The Cardinals' three MVP candidates, Albert Pujols, Scott Rolen and Jim Edmonds, were a combined 6-for-45 (.133) with no home runs and one RBI.

"They outplayed us in every category, so it ended up not being a terrific competition," Cardinals manager Tony La Russa said.

Game 4 began like the others in this series, with the Red Sox establishing themselves in the first. Johnny Damon hit Jason Marquis' fourth pitch over the

Johnny Damon, the game's first batter, made it perfectly clear that a sweeping change was about to grip the baseball world. Several hours later, the Red Sox stormed the field and championship dreams became reality.

ST. LOUIS 000 000 000 | 0 4 0 L: MARQUIS (0-1, 3.86)

right field wall. It also was Damon who set the tone for the Sox's ALCS-clinching win over the Yankees with two home runs and six RBIs in Game 7.

The Red Sox threatened to get to Marquis again in the second. Trot Nixon hit a one-out double, and Mark Bellhorn walked. A sacrifice by Derek Lowe moved both runners up 90 feet, but Damon grounded out to first. Then in the third, Manny Ramirez had a one-out single and David Ortiz followed with a double. Jason Varitek hit a hard grounder to first, and Pujols, who was playing back, fired home to nail Ramirez, giving Marquis another chance to escape damage.

But Bill Mueller walked on four pitches, and Nixon took three straight balls. Instead of playing it safe and taking a pitch, the Sox turned Nixon loose. Knowing that Marquis would groove one, Nixon pounced and laced a ball off the right-center field wall. He just missed a grand slam, but Ortiz and Varitek scored, and the lead grew to 3-0. That, as it turned out, was the last run the Sox scored—the last run anybody scored in the 2004 baseball season.

That's because Lowe pretty much took care of things from there. He was the third straight Sox starter to not allow an earned run, and he had the Redbirds eating out of his hand through seven innings, allowing three hits and a walk and striking out four.

Angst-filled Red Sox fans kept waiting for something bad to happen … and kept waiting … and kept waiting. Bronson Arroyo allowed a one-out walk to Reggie Sanders in the eighth, but reliever Alan Embree struck out pinch hitter Hector Luna and got Larry Walker on a popup to shortstop Orlando Cabrera.

After Foulke took over in the ninth, a leadoff single by Pujols stoked the hope of Cardinals fans and the nerves of the Boston faithful. But Foulke retired Rolen, who went hitless in the series, on a fly ball to right, then struck out

Jason Marquis was solid for the Cardinals, but Derek Lowe was terrific for the Red Sox. Lowe received sufficient offensive support from Johnny Damon (right), who homered in the first, and David Ortiz (below).

Nixon: 3-for-4, 2 RBIs

Edmonds on three pitches. All that was left was Renteria, and on a 1-0 pitch, he bounced back to Foulke, who ran halfway to first, then tossed the World Series victory ball to Doug Mientkiewicz—and the party was on. Foulke headed for Varitek, and those two embraced on the infield, and it didn't take long for the rest of the Sox to engulf them.

The celebration was filled with ecstacy, but also outlined with relief—relief that no longer would the Red Sox be known as cursed. Instead, they were champs.

"Any time you don a Red Sox uniform, you have to talk about the history of this team and not having a World Series championship since 1918," said Nixon, the longest-tenured Sox player. "1918 is gone forever. We're not going to have to hear about that again. I'm sure the people back in Boston are so happy."

And thankful that the so-called "curse" finally had been lifted.

Cardinals catcher Yadier Molina tags out Manny Ramirez (right) and then has a heated discussion with him (below) during a later Ramirez at-bat. The topic of their discourse was never revealed.

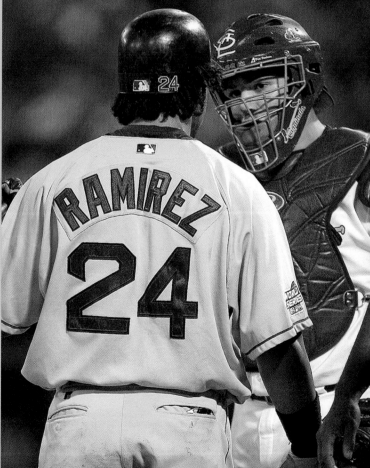

Trot Nixon, swinging at a 3-0 pitch with the bases loaded, delivered a two-run double off the right-center field wall.

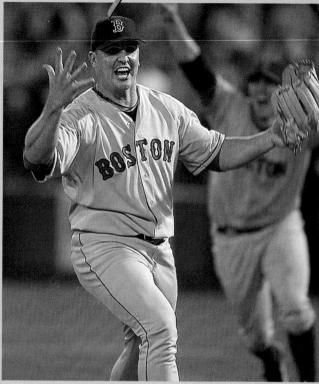

Derek Lowe got a 'well done' from catcher Jason Varitek, and Keith Foulke (above right) got the chance to celebrate on center stage. The fans were swept up in the excitement.

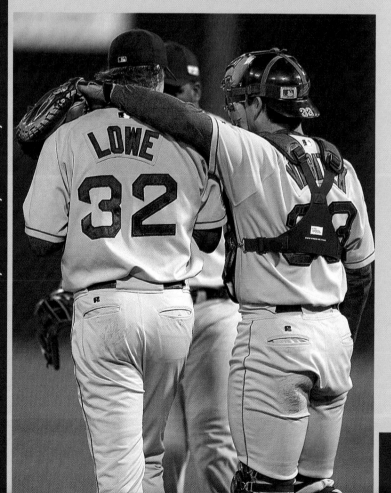

Lowe: 7 IP, 3 H, 0 R, 4 SO

Lowe flies high in postseason

During the last weekend of the regular season, Sox manager Terry Francona informed Derek Lowe he wouldn't be a part of the team's postseason rotation.

"We told him he had a day to pout, yell or whatever," Francona said. "But he didn't pout. He got himself ready and look at what he did."

Look, indeed.

Lowe picked up the win by pitching a scoreless 10th inning in deciding Game 3 of the A.L. Division Series against Anaheim. Back in the rotation for the A.L. Championship Series, Lowe beat the Yankees with a masterful performance in Game 7.

And then in Game 4 of the World Series, Lowe shut out the Cardinals on three hits over seven innings.

Three series-clinching wins. Not bad for a guy who had his nose pressed to the glass of Boston's rotation entering the playoffs.

Against the Cardinals, Lowe allowed a leadoff single to Tony Womack but then used a sharp sinker to help him retire the next 13 Cardinals in order. Meanwhile, the Sox built their lead.

When the Cardinals' Edgar Renteria reached third with one out in the fifth, Lowe reached down and produced one of his four strikeouts to keep St. Louis scoreless. He left for a pinch hitter in the top of the eighth, and the Sox's bullpen protected his win and the shutout.

Lowe's tenure with Boston was star-crossed. He was an inconsistent closer, then a dominant starter, especially in 2002 when he won 21 games and threw a no-hitter. But he largely was ineffective in 2004, winning 14 games and compiling a 5.42 ERA.

Whether struggling or starring, the happy-go-lucky Lowe stayed positive and was a big part of a close-knit team that played hard but loose.

"We're pretty proud of him," Francona said. "Our guys love him so much. For him to be out there was really, really neat."

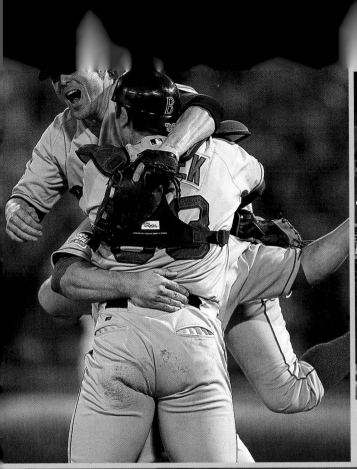

Red Sox Nation had plenty of heroes to embrace, including Curt Schilling (above) and Pedro Martinez (below). Hugs and champagne were the order of the night.

Game 1   April 4   Orioles 7, Red Sox 2   0-1

Pedro's first game since his ALCS Game 7 meltdown doesn't go well, as O's newcomer Javy Lopez hits a homer, double on a cold Sunday night.

Game 2   April 6   Red Sox 4, Orioles 1   1-1

Schilling pays immediate dividends with a six-inning, seven-strikeout debut, which is punctuated by Foulke's first Red Sox save.

Game 3   April 7   Red Sox 10, Orioles 3   2-1

Damon, Mueller, Ramirez, Ortiz, Millar—Sox demonstrate quick-strike capabilities in seven-run second inning.

Game 4   April 8   Orioles 3, Red Sox 2 (13)   2-2

Wild thing: Bobby Jones walks four batters in unlucky 13th after Burks ties game in the sixth with his last major league home run.

Game 5   April 9   Blue Jays 10, Red Sox 5   2-3

Sleepy Sox, whose charter did not get into Boston until 6:37 a.m., doze off as Jays score three in the eighth and three in the ninth of Fenway opener.

Game 6   April 10   Red Sox 4, Blue Jays 1   3-3

The 'old Pedro' puts on a show with 7⅔ innings of four-hit ball, Foulke gets first Fenway save, and Ramirez, Bellhorn and Ortiz homer.

Game 7   April 11   Red Sox 6, Blue Jays 4 (12)   4-3

Bellhorn ties game with a single in the ninth, and Ortiz tames the Monster with his first walkoff homer in 12th.

Game 8   April 15   Orioles 12, Red Sox 7 (11)   4-4

After a day off and two straight rainouts, Sox commit two throwing errors in 11th inning and Orioles score five runs.

Game 9   April 16   Red Sox 6, Yankees 2   5-4

Rivalry 2004 attracts a national TV crowd, a rarity for a Friday in April. Wakefield's knuckleball flutters through seven strong innings.

Game 10   April 17   Red Sox 5, Yankees 2   6-4

Schilling shines, Manny homers, and A-Rod struggles as Sox beat the Yanks again. Ramirez's fifth-inning blast is career No. 350.

Game 11   April 18   Yankees 7, Red Sox 3   6-5

The Empire strikes back, taking control in a six-run third inning that features RBIs from six different Yankees. Lowe is the victim.

Game 12   April 19   Red Sox 5, Yankees 4   7-5

Kapler's clutch single in eighth secures a Patriots Day victory and a 3-1 series win. Ortiz goes 3-for-4 and knocks in the tying run in the seventh.

Game 13   April 20   Red Sox 4, Blue Jays 2   8-5

In a Cy Young matchup, Martinez allows five hits in seven innings and outduels Roy Halladay. Varitek, Ortiz get three hits apiece.

Game 14   April 21   Red Sox 4, Blue Jays 2   9-5

It's Mirabelli time in Toronto as the backup catcher hits two homers, drives in three runs in support of Wakefield, Foulke.

Game 15   April 22   Blue Jays 7, Red Sox 3   9-6

The day before Boston's first 2004 game at Yankee Stadium, Schilling gives up eighth-inning slam to Chris Gomez and gets his first loss in Sox uniform.

Game 16   April 23   Red Sox 11, Yankees 2   10-6

The ghost of ALCS past is exorcised, temporarily at least, with a four-home run explosion and the pitching of Lowe.

Game 17   April 24   Red Sox 3, Yankees 2 (12)   11-6

Bellhorn's sacrifice fly, the team's third in this small-ball game, moves the Red Sox a half game ahead of the Yankees in A.L. East.

Game 18   April 25   Red Sox 2, Yankees 0   12-6

Pedro throws seven shutout innings, and Ramirez hits a two-run homer to give Sox their first Yankee Stadium sweep since 1999.

Game 19   April 28   Red Sox 6, Devil Rays 0   13-6

The battery-charged Sox get a home run from Varitek and five-hit ball over 7⅓ innings from Schilling en route to their second straight shutout win.

Game 20   April 29   Red Sox 4, Devil Rays 0   14-6

Kim is near perfect in his five-inning, one-hit season debut, and the Sox stretch their scoreless-innings streak to 32.

Game 21   April 29   Red Sox 7, Devil Rays 3   15-6

Devil Rays snap Red Sox scoreless-innings streak with two runs in first, but Sox score seven in their first at-bat to sweep this doubleheader.

Game 22   May 1   Rangers 4, Red Sox 3   15-7

Three-run rally in seventh off Malaska and Williamson snaps the bullpen's 32⅓-inning scoreless streak in opener of doubleheader.

Game 23   May 1   Rangers 8, Red Sox 5   15-8

A double dose of disappointment: Pedro gets knocked around as Rangers complete twin killing.

Game 24   May 2   Rangers 4, Red Sox 1   15-9

R.A. Dickey shuts down Red Sox for broom-wielding Rangers fan. The only run scores on Varitek's bases-loaded walk in ninth inning.

Game 25   May 3   Indians 2, Red Sox 1   15-10

Two-run Victor Martinez home run off Schilling in first is all the Indians need to beat the suddenly offense-challenged Red Sox.

Game 26   May 4   Indians 7, Red Sox 6   15-11

Four-run ninth-inning rally, fueled by Damon's three-run homer, falls short as Ramirez, representing the potential lead run, strikes out to end game.

Game 27   May 5   Red Sox 9, Indians 5   16-11

Ortiz has a blast—two of them, in fact—as the Red Sox snap a five-game losing streak behind 5⅔ innings of scoreless relief from five pitchers.

Game 28   May 6   Red Sox 5, Indians 2   17-11

Pedro pitches and Manny homers, but Pokey grabs the spotlight by delivering key double in a two-run seventh-inning rally.

Game 29   May 7   Red Sox 7, Royals 6   18-11

Five runs in the last two innings, including Varitek's double to chase home Manny with the game-winner, save Red Sox from Royal embarrassment.

Game 30   May 8   Red Sox 9, Royals 1   19-11

Schilling strikes out eight and goes the distance as Reese hits two homers—including an inside-the-park shot—in Red Sox's fourth straight win.

Game 31   May 9   Royals 8, Red Sox 4   19-12

Pokey giveth, Pokey taketh away: Error allows two runs as opportunistic Royals show Lowe how they can go.

Game 32   May 10   Indians 10, Red Sox 6   19-13

Poor outing by Kim angers Fenway faithful, prompts Red Sox to give Arroyo his spot in rotation; Daubach hits first home run.

Game 33   May 11   Red Sox 5, Indians 3   20-13

McCarty's star rises over Fenway, thanks to a two-run, eighth-inning triple that makes a winner out of Embree and sets up Foulke's seventh save.

Game 34   May 12   Indians 6, Red Sox 4   20-14

Wakefield struggles, and the first-place Red Sox stagger to their fourth loss in seven games against the surprising Indians.

Game 35   May 13   Blue Jays 12, Red Sox 6   20-15

Errors of their ways: Gaffes by DiNardo, Damon lead to five Jays runs in the sixth as the Red Sox fall out of first for the first time since April 23.

Game 36   May 14   Red Sox 9, Blue Jays 3   21-15

Millar, Daubach, Crespo, Ortiz come through in a six-run eighth that puts Red Sox back on winning track.

Game 37   May 15   Red Sox 4, Blue Jays 0   22-15

Arroyo works eight outstanding innings, and Youkilis becomes first Red Sox player to homer in his major league debut since Sam Horn in 1987.

Game 38   May 16   Blue Jays 3, Red Sox 1   22-16

In a Cy Young reprise, Halladay avenges earlier loss to Pedro, but surprising Youkilis goes 2-for-4 for second straight game.

Game 39   May 18   Red Sox 7, Devil Rays 3   23-16

Who's your daddy? Wakefield, celebrating the birth of his son, goes seven innings in his 400th career game, and Sox move back into first place.

Game 40   May 19   Red Sox 4, Devil Rays 1   24-16

Schilling cruises to his fifth win and becomes the fourth active pitcher to reach 2,600 strikeouts when he fans Aubrey Huff in the fourth inning.

Game 41   **May 20**   **Devil Rays 9, Red Sox 6**   **24-17**
Down 7-0, thanks to more Lowe struggles, Sox pull to within 7-6, thanks to nine walks. But Devil Rays bullpen helps Yankees regain first place.

Game 42   **May 21**   **Red Sox 11, Blue Jays 5**   **25-17**
Red Sox continue their big-inning ways with a six-run, eighth-inning explosion that moves them back into first place.

Game 43   **May 22**   **Red Sox 5, Blue Jays 2**   **26-17**
Blue Jays get a double dose of Martinez as Pedro works six strong innings and Anastacio wins in relief, thanks to Bellhorn's seventh-inning single.

Game 44   **May 23**   **Red Sox 7, Blue Jays 2**   **27-17**
Blue Jays knuckle under again as Red Sox score early and often and Wakefield flutters through seven strong innings.

Game 45   **May 25**   **Red Sox 12, Athletics 2**   **28-17**
Ortiz and Bellhorn combine for seven hits, seven RBIs and six runs. Schilling shines, while the A's Tim Hudson gets hammered.

Game 46   **May 26**   **Red Sox 9, Athletics 6**   **29-17**
Two-out, fourth-inning error by A's shortstop Bobby Crosby opens door for five runs to hand Lowe a victory, albeit a wobbly one.

Game 47   **May 27**   **Athletics 15, Red Sox 2**   **29-18**
Arroyo gets battered, and Red Sox get a dose of their own offensive medicine as A's score three or more runs in four different innings.

Game 48   **May 28**   **Red Sox 8, Mariners 4**   **30-18**
Ortiz hits a grand slam, and Youkilis drives in three runs to give a shaky Pedro his fifth win of season.

Game 49   **May 29**   **Mariners 5, Red Sox 4**   **30-19**
Five early runs doom Wakefield and Red Sox, who slip a half game behind the Yankees despite getting a homer by Ramirez.

Game 50   **May 30**   **Red Sox 9, Mariners 7 (12)**   **31-19**
In a 'Who are those guys?' scenario, McCarty delivers a walkoff homer off J.J. Putz in the 12th inning to give a win to Anastacio Martinez.

Game 51   **May 31**   **Orioles 13, Red Sox 4**   **31-20**
The Orioles rough up Lowe and drop Red Sox into first-place tie with Yankees. This marks the last time the Sox sit atop the A.L. East in 2004.

Game 52   **June 1**   **Angels 7, Red Sox 6**   **31-21**
Ramirez and Varitek get three hits apiece, and Daubach and Millar homer, but Angels rock Arroyo and please 43,285 fans at Angel Stadium.

Game 53   **June 2**   **Angels 10, Red Sox 7**   **31-22**
Vlad is bad: Angels get four hits, two home runs and nine RBIs from Guerrero in a come-from-behind victory over Sox. Pedro is bad, too.

Game 54   **June 4**   **Royals 5, Red Sox 2**   **31-23**
Mirabelli homer is only bright spot as Royals Gobble up Wakefield and hand Red Sox their fourth straight loss.

Game 55   **June 5**   **Red Sox 8, Royals 4**   **32-23**
Schilling halts the skid, and Sox lash out 13 hits, including home runs by Youkilis, Bellhorn and Ortiz.

Game 56   **June 6**   **Red Sox 5, Royals 3**   **33-23**
Backups Kapler, Crespo and Reese step up big as Red Sox post first back-to-back victories since May 25-26.

Game 57   **June 8**   **Red Sox 1, Padres 0**   **34-23**
Interleague play begins: Pedro gets ninth-inning help from Foulke as Red Sox record their first 1-0 win since July 23, 2000.

Game 58   **June 9**   **Padres 8, Red Sox 1**   **34-24**
Nomar returns and gets a hit, but the Padres, behind Brian Lawrence, survive a long rain delay to post their first-ever victory at Fenway Park.

Game 59   **June 10**   **Red Sox 9, Padres 3**   **35-24**
Bad move: Padres, leading 3-1 in fifth, walk Ramirez intentionally to face Garciaparra with the bases loaded. Nomar doubles off the left field wall.

Game 60   **June 11**   **Red Sox 2, Dodgers 1**   **36-24**
Ortiz's game-ending single in ninth bails out Ramirez, who allowed the tying run to score in top of the inning by dropping a routine fly ball.

Game 61   **June 12**   **Dodgers 14, Red Sox 5**   **36-25**
After the Dodgers scored 13 runs in the fourth, fifth and sixth, Francona gets welcome relief from McCarty, who retires the side in order in ninth.

Game 62   **June 13**   **Red Sox 4, Dodgers 1**   **37-25**
In a Sunday night game, Reese doubles home two fourth-inning runs, and the Red Sox send the Dodgers packing with two losses in three games.

Game 63   **June 15**   **Rockies 6, Red Sox 3**   **37-26**
In their first game ever at Coors Field, the Red Sox lose to the Rockies, who get home runs from Vinny Castilla and Todd Helton.

Game 64   **June 16**   **Rockies 7, Red Sox 6**   **37-27**
Schilling gets roughed up, and the Red Sox lose again at Coors, despite getting a homer from Nixon in his season debut after a back injury.

Game 65   **June 17**   **Red Sox 11, Rockies 0**   **38-27**
A Rocky Mountain Lowe: Righthander pitches seven shutout innings, and Red Sox avoid sweep behind Ortiz's five RBIs.

Game 66   **June 18**   **Red Sox 14, Giants 9**   **39-27**
Ortiz, Ramirez, Millar, Nixon and Mirabelli hit home runs as Red Sox overcome 7-2 deficit with seven-run, fifth-inning explosion.

Game 67   **June 19**   **Giants 6, Red Sox 4**   **39-28**
After the Sox tie game with three eighth-inning runs, the Giants strike back in the bottom of the inning on Edgardo Alfonzo's two-run homer off Embree.

Game 68   **June 20**   **Giants 4, Red Sox 0**   **39-29**
One hit! Youkilis' sixth-inning double is only safety off Jason Schmidt, who is supported by Alfonzo's seventh-inning grand slam off Timlin.

Game 69   **June 22**   **Red Sox 9, Twins 2**   **40-29**
Following an intentional walk to Ortiz, Garciaparra hits a grand slam—his first homer of the season—to straightaway center.

Game 70   **June 23**   **Twins 4, Red Sox 2**   **40-30**
Homers by Nixon, Bellhorn provide Red Sox with their only runs in a game that is decided by a Torii Hunter blast off Lowe in the sixth.

Game 71   **June 24**   **Twins 4, Red Sox 3 (10)**   **40-31**
Garciaparra's throwing error in the 10th enables Cristian Guzman to reach base, and he eventually scores on a Lew Ford sacrifice fly.

Game 72   **June 25**   **Red Sox 12, Phillies 1**   **41-31**
Pedro is brilliant, and the Red Sox offense gets eight in the sixth to cruise to a rain-shortened win. Ramirez and Youkilis combine for nine RBIs.

Game 73   **June 26**   **Phillies 9, Red Sox 2**   **41-32**
Defenseless Red Sox make four errors, and Phillies score five unearned runs. Jim Thome burns Arroyo for major league-leading 26th home run.

Game 74   **June 27**   **Red Sox 12, Phillies 3**   **42-32**
Prepping for another visit to New York, the Red Sox post two four-run innings and hand Schilling his 10th victory.

Game 75   **June 29**   **Yankees 11, Red Sox 3**   **42-33**
Three costly errors, two by Garciaparra, lead to four unearned runs and a Yankee win. Damon homers twice, once into Yankee Stadium's upper deck.

Game 76   **June 30**   **Yankees 4, Red Sox 2**   **42-34**
E-2: Ortiz's bases-loaded muff and Garciaparra's wild throw give the Yankees another win and a 7½-game lead over the second-place Sox.

Game 77   **July 1**   **Yankees 5, Red Sox 4 (13)**   **42-35**
Who can forget Derek Jeter diving into the stands to make a catch in the 12th? Ramirez homers in 13th, but Yankees score two in bottom of inning.

Game 78   **July 2**   **Braves 6, Red Sox 3 (12)**   **42-36**
Rookie Nick Green hits a three-run homer in the 12th inning off Anastacio Martinez to send the Red Sox to their second straight heartbreaking loss.

Game 79   **July 3**   **Red Sox 6, Braves 1**   **43-36**
Schilling goes the distance, strikes out 10 and ends the Sox's four-game losing streak. Mirabelli provides the big blow with a sixth-inning grand slam.

Game 80   **July 4**   **Braves 10, Red Sox 4**   **43-37**
The Braves give Turner Field fans an on-field fireworks display—nine runs in the fifth inning, with most of the damage coming against Lowe.

Game 81   **July 6**   **Red Sox 11, Athletics 0**   **44-37**
Mueller goes deep, Damon goes shallow, and Wakefield goes seven solid innings. Mueller hits a homer, and Damon contributes five singles.

Game 82   **July 7**   **Red Sox 11, Athletics 3**   **45-37**
22-3: That's the two-day tally against the shellshocked A's as Pedro wins for a ninth time and Ramirez, Garciaparra and Bellhorn hit home runs.

Game 83   July 8   Red Sox 8, Athletics 7 (10)   46-37
After blowing a 7-1 lead, the Red Sox complete their three-game sweep when Mueller doubles home Damon in the 10th inning.

Game 84   July 9   Red Sox 7, Rangers 0   47-37
Arroyo, ending his six-game losing streak, zeroes in for eight innings as Damon goes 4-for-5 with two homers and four RBIs.

Game 85   July 10   Red Sox 14, Rangers 6   48-37
The Red Sox, with Ramirez belting two home runs, unleash a 21-hit attack and score seven or more runs for the fifth straight game.

Game 86   July 11   Rangers 6, Red Sox 5   48-38
The Red Sox, who see their five-game winning streak come to an end, enter the All-Star break seven games behind the Yankees.

Game 87   July 15   Angels 8, Red Sox 1   48-39
West Coast swing begins with a thud. Angels ride a five-run fifth and the pitching of Jarrod Washburn to an easy victory.

Game 88   July 16   Red Sox 4, Angels 2   49-39
Nomar and Pedro: Just like the good old days, Martinez gets the win (his 10th), and Garciaparra homers (his fifth) as the Red Sox roll.

Game 89   July 17   Angels 8, Red Sox 3   49-40
Wakefield takes a Jose Molina line drive off the back and leaves the game—providing relief in more ways than one.

Game 90   July 18   Red Sox 6, Angels 2   50-40
Ortiz's three-run homer provides all the support Schilling needs en route to his 12th victory in 16 decisions.

Game 91   July 19   Mariners 8, Red Sox 4 (11)   50-41
Boone revisited: This time brother Bret does the dirty work with a walkoff grand slam off Leskanic in the 11th inning.

Game 92   July 20   Red Sox 9, Mariners 7   51-41
Red Sox score eight runs in the fourth inning and hold on, with Foulke halting the Mariners' rally in the ninth for his 15th save.

Game 93   July 21   Orioles 10, Red Sox 5   51-42
Homecoming is not so sweet for the Red Sox and Pedro, who suffers his fourth loss and allows two three-run innings.

Game 94   July 22   Orioles 8, Red Sox 3   51-43
Orioles ruin the major league debut of lefty Abe Alvarez, the first Red Sox pitcher to jump from Class AA since 2001, in the opener of a doubleheader.

Game 95   July 22   Red Sox 4, Orioles 0   52-43
Red Sox gain a split behind Wakefield, who works seven scoreless innings, and Youkilis, who hits his fourth home run.

Game 96   July 23   Yankees 8, Red Sox 7   52-44
Millar hits three home runs, but Ruthian efforts are not enough to slow down the Yankee express, which increases its lead to 9½ games.

Game 97   July 24   Red Sox 11, Yankees 10   53-44
A baseball classic, which features a third-inning brawl, ends when Mueller hits a two-run, ninth-inning homer off Yankee closer Mariano Rivera.

Game 98   July 25   Red Sox 9, Yankees 6   54-44
Feeding off the previous day's excitement, the Sox get homers from Millar, Bellhorn and Damon and trim the Yankees' lead to 7½ games.

Game 99   July 26   Red Sox 12, Orioles 5   55-44
Martinez gives up five runs in 6⅓ innings but still improves to 11-4 as Sox deliver the goods in a six-run third inning.

Game 100   July 28   Orioles 4, Red Sox 1   55-45
Schilling is outpitched by Orioles prospect Dave Borkowski, who allows three hits in seven innings. Javy Lopez homers twice against Schilling.

Game 101   July 30   Red Sox 8, Twins 2   56-45
Kapler and Ortiz combine for six of the Red Sox's 16 hits, and Arroyo is solid for 7⅓ innings in a game played at the Metrodome.

Game 102   July 31   Twins 5, Red Sox 4   56-46
A momentous day: Garciaparra is gone, and Cabrera, Mientkiewicz and Roberts are in as trading-deadline deals overshadow a month-ending loss.

Game 103   August 1   Twins 4, Red Sox 3   56-47
Johan Santana outpitches Martinez in a loss that features new shortstop Cabrera's first Red Sox home run.

Game 104   August 2   Red Sox 6, Devil Rays 3   57-47
McCarty's three-run homer is the difference for the Red Sox and Wakefield, who works seven innings and picks up his seventh win.

Game 105   August 3   Red Sox 5, Devil Rays 2   58-47
Schilling, thanks to three RBIs by Mueller and a home run by Varitek, posts his third complete game and 13th victory.

Game 106   August 4   Devil Rays 5, Red Sox 4   58-48
Pinch runner Roberts, trying to score on a Mientkiewicz single, is gunned out at the plate in the ninth, providing a dramatic conclusion to the series.

Game 107   August 6   Tigers 4, Red Sox 3   58-49
Varitek homers, and Lowe works seven solid innings, but the Sox can't muster enough offense to win the opener at Comerica Park.

Game 108   August 7   Red Sox 7, Tigers 4   59-49
Pedro strikes out 11 in seven innings, records his 12th win and helps the Red Sox snap a two-game losing streak.

Game 109   August 8   Red Sox 11, Tigers 9   60-49
Two home runs by Youkilis and another by Ortiz power the Sox. Wakefield becomes the first pitcher since 1932 to give up six homers and still win.

Game 110   August 9   Devil Rays 8, Red Sox 3   60-50
Devil Rays score seven runs in fifth and sixth innings, six off Schilling, in a forgettable loss to open a 10-game homestand.

Game 111   August 10   Red Sox 8, Devil Rays 4   61-50
Arroyo, with solid relief from Myers, Adams and Foulke, puts Sox back on winning track in an unusual homerless game at Fenway Park.

Game 112   August 11   Red Sox 14, Devil Rays 4   62-50
Millar (a homer and 4 RBIs) and Damon (2 RBIs) go 7-for-7 in a one-sided game the Red Sox lead 13-1 after three innings.

Game 113   August 12   Red Sox 6, Devil Rays 0   63-50
For the first time since September 2003, Pedro pitches a complete game, stopping the Rays on six hits while striking out 10. Youkilis homers.

Game 114   August 13   White Sox 8, Red Sox 7   63-51
Former Yankee Jose Contreras survives three-run second inning and beats Red Sox, despite a two-run, ninth-inning homer by Millar.

Game 115   August 14   Red Sox 4, White Sox 3   64-51
After giving up first-inning homers to Timo Perez and Carlos Lee, Schilling works eight and gets 14th win. Ramirez, Ortiz hit back-to-back shots.

Game 116   August 15   White Sox 5, Red Sox 4   64-52
Ninth-inning two-run single by Varitek is too little, too late as Boston drops two of three to the other Sox.

Game 117   August 16   Red Sox 8, Blue Jays 4   65-52
Lowe gets 11th win, Foulke gets 20th save, and Sox begin an incredible 17-game run in which they win 16 and pull within 2½ games of Yankees.

Game 118   August 17   Red Sox 5, Blue Jays 4   66-52
Struggling Cabrera bounces a ninth-inning double off the Green Monster scoreboard, scoring Damon and giving the Sox instant victory.

Game 119   August 18   Red Sox 6, Blue Jays 4   67-52
It's cruise control for Wakefield, who works eight solid innings after Sox stake him to a 4-0 first-inning lead on RBIs by Millar, Cabrera and Mueller.

Game 120   August 20   Red Sox 10, White Sox 1   68-52
Ramirez's grand slam, Cabrera's four RBIs and Schilling's seven innings of shutout pitching start a six-game trip off in style.

Game 121   August 21   Red Sox 10, White Sox 7   69-52
The big bats of Ramirez (five RBIs) and Varitek (two homers) help make up for the shaky pitching of Arroyo, who still picks up his sixth win.

Game 122   August 22   Red Sox 6, White Sox 5   70-52
Ramirez and Ortiz show their formidable 1-2 punch as they go back to back in the eighth inning to erase a 5-4 deficit.

Game 123   **August 23**   **Blue Jays 3, Red Sox 0**   **70-53**
The Sox can't touch Ted Lilly, who allows only three hits, fans 13 and ends Boston's six-game win streak. Only Cabrera and Bellhorn reach base.

Game 124   **August 24**   **Red Sox 5, Blue Jays 4**   **71-53**
Timlin pitches out of a bases-loaded, no-out jam in the fifth, and Mirabelli, filling in for the suspended Varitek, smashes a three-run homer in the sixth.

Game 125   **August 25**   **Red Sox 11, Blue Jays 5**   **72-53**
Ortiz leads a 17-hit attack with three hits, two homers and four RBIs. That's more than enough for Schilling, who wins his 16th.

Game 126   **August 26**   **Red Sox 4, Tigers 1**   **73-53**
Arroyo rebounds from a rough start with a gem: 7⅓ innings, one run, eight strikeouts. Timlin and Foulke are perfect in finishing.

Game 127   **August 27**   **Red Sox 5, Tigers 3**   **74-53**
Lowe continues his trend of strong starts by working a season-high eight innings. Gutierrez gets a rare start—and three hits and two RBIs.

Game 128   **August 28**   **Red Sox 5, Tigers 1**   **75-53**
After being a tough-luck loser against Lilly his last time out, there's no denying Pedro against the Tigers, as he allows one run in seven innings.

Game 129   **August 29**   **Red Sox 6, Tigers 1**   **76-53**
Wakefield is strong for the Sox, who limit the Tigers to six runs in the four-game sweep. Ramirez drives in two in the Sox's four-run fifth.

Game 130   **August 31**   **Red Sox 10, Angels 7**   **77-53**
In a showdown between wild-card contenders, the Sox build a 10-1 lead—and then have to hold off the Angels. Manny goes deep twice.

Game 131   **Sept. 1**   **Red Sox 12, Angels 7**   **78-53**
Two of the best offenses in baseball flex their muscles. Every Sox starter gets a hit, led by Damon's four, and Millar hits a three-run homer.

Game 132   **Sept. 2**   **Red Sox 4, Angels 3**   **79-53**
Lowe struggles early, then settles down as the wild-card lead over the Angels increases to 4½ games. This is the Sox's 15th win in 16 games.

Game 133   **Sept. 3**   **Red Sox 2, Rangers 0**   **80-53**
Pedro throws seven shutout innings to silence the Rangers' big bats. The 10th straight win moves the Sox to within 2½ of the Yankees.

Game 134   **Sept. 4**   **Rangers 8, Red Sox 6**   **80-54**
The winning streak comes to an end, as Wakefield allows eight runs in six innings, though Bellhorn's grand slam in the seventh adds some drama.

Game 135   **Sept. 5**   **Red Sox 6, Rangers 5**   **81-54**
Schilling gets the team back on the winning track by pitching into the ninth, though four Rangers runs in that frame make things interesting.

Game 136   **Sept. 6**   **Red Sox 8, Athletics 3**   **82-54**
RBI doubles by Mueller and Roberts break a 2-2 seventh-inning tie, and the Sox add four in the ninth, three on a double by Ortiz.

Game 137   **Sept. 7**   **Red Sox 7, Athletics 1**   **83-54**
Damon returns after missing four games and leads off the game with a homer. Lowe wins his 14th by allowing one run in 6⅓ innings.

Game 138   **Sept. 8**   **Red Sox 8, Athletics 3**   **84-54**
The Sox pull to within two games of the Yankees by pounding Hudson for the second time this season.

Game 139   **Sept. 9**   **Mariners 7, Red Sox 1**   **84-55**
Sloppy, sloppy, sloppy. Two errors, five unearned runs, a passed ball and a balk help topple the Sox, who don't score until the ninth.

Game 140   **Sept. 10**   **Red Sox 13, Mariners 2**   **85-55**
Ramirez and Ortiz homer in the same game for the 12th time this season. Manny's second of the game is a grand slam—and his 40th of the season.

Game 141   **Sept. 11**   **Red Sox 9, Mariners 0**   **86-55**
Ramirez homers again, but the real headliner is Arroyo, who throws seven scoreless innings. Bellhorn's two-run homer highlights a four-run fifth.

Game 142   **Sept. 12**   **Mariners 2, Red Sox 0**   **86-56**
The Sox only manage a split against the woeful M's, as Gil Meche shuts down Boston's bats. Raul Ibanez's two-run homer supplies the only runs.

Game 143   **Sept. 14**   **Devil Rays 5, Red Sox 2**   **86-57**
Scott Kazmir, the youngest player in the majors at 20 years, 7 months, stops the Sox on three hits over six innings. Nixon hits a two-run pinch-hit homer.

Game 144   **Sept. 15**   **Red Sox 8, Devil Rays 6**   **87-57**
Red Sox win ugly as Millar, Bellhorn homer and Francona employs six pitchers. Millar's homer is career No. 100.

Game 145   **Sept. 16**   **Red Sox 11, Devil Rays 4**   **88-57**
Damon, Millar each homer, drive in four to help Schilling lift his Fenway Park record to 11-1 and become the major leagues' first 20-game winner.

Game 146   **Sept. 17**   **Red Sox 3, Yankees 2**   **89-57**
Cabrera, Damon drive in ninth-inning runs off Mariano Rivera, and Foulke gets his 30th save as Sox trim Yankees' lead to 2½ games.

Game 147   **Sept. 18**   **Yankees 14, Red Sox 4**   **89-58**
Lowe gives up seven runs before recording an out in the second, and Jon Lieber flirts with a no-hitter before Ortiz hits a two-out homer in seventh.

Game 148   **Sept. 19**   **Yankees 11, Red Sox 1**   **89-59**
Yankees rout Pedro, win two of three games in the series and reassert their control over the Red Sox in A.L. East Division.

Game 149   **Sept. 20**   **Orioles 9, Red Sox 6**   **89-60**
Eight Baltimore runs in fourth and fifth doom Sox to their first three-game losing streak since early July. Sox are 1-5 vs. Orioles at Fenway Park.

Game 150   **Sept. 21**   **Red Sox 3, Orioles 2**   **90-60**
Orioles take lead on two-run Lopez homer in ninth off Foulke. Sox win it in the bottom of the ninth on Bellhorn's two-run single.

Game 151   **Sept. 22**   **Red Sox 7, Orioles 6 (12)**   **91-60**
Cabrera rescues Sox with 12th-inning home run after Foulke blows save in ninth for second straight night. Leskanic gets fifth win in relief.

Game 152   **Sept. 23**   **Orioles 9, Red Sox 7**   **91-61**
Pitching plagues Red Sox, who get shaky efforts from Lowe, Myers and Kim. Ramirez's two-run single in the ninth makes game close.

Game 153   **Sept. 24**   **Yankees 6, Red Sox 4**   **91-62**
Hideki Matsui homer, Ruben Sierra single doom Martinez in eighth. Frustrated Pedro calls Yankees 'my daddy,' a comment that will haunt him in ALCS.

Game 154   **Sept. 25**   **Red Sox 12, Yankees 5**   **92-62**
Two-run Mirabelli double highlights seven-run eighth inning that ensures Yankees will not clinch A.L. East title at Fenway Park.

Game 155   **Sept. 26**   **Red Sox 11, Yankees 4**   **93-62**
Red Sox blast Kevin Brown, and Schilling allows one hit in seven innings en route to 21st win. Game includes another bench-clearing incident.

Game 156   **Sept. 27**   **Red Sox 7, Devil Rays 3**   **94-62**
Damon, Ramirez, Varitek, McCarty all homer in support of Arroyo as the Red Sox clinch the A.L. wild-card berth.

Game 157   **Sept. 28**   **Red Sox 10, Devil Rays 8 (11)**   **95-62**
Millar's two-run homer in the top of the 11th produces Boston's fourth straight win after five relievers shut out Devil Rays over final six innings.

Game 158   **Sept. 29**   **Devil Rays 9, Red Sox 4**   **95-63**
Pedro is routed again in his career-high fourth straight loss as Tino Martinez breaks open the game with a three-run, eighth-inning homer off Embree.

Game 159   **October 1**   **Red Sox 8, Orioles 3**   **96-63**
Damon hits career-high 20th homer, Ortiz hits three-run shot in the ninth, and Wakefield records 12th victory with six solid innings.

Game 160   **October 2**   **Red Sox 7, Orioles 5**   **97-63**
Six-run second, capped by Damon's two-run single, propels Sox past O's in opener of doubleheader. Burks plays in his 2,000th career game.

Game 161   **October 2**   **Red Sox 7, Orioles 5**   **98-63**
Cabrera's three-run homer in sixth, Mientkiewicz's two-run triple in seventh lift Sox to doubleheader sweep and Kim to first win since April 29.

Game 162   **October 3**   **Orioles 3, Red Sox 2**   **98-64**
As many regulars rest or leave game early, Red Sox lose season finale. Nixon, Damon drive in Boston's final runs of the regular season.